BISHOP ALMA WHITE, A. M.

Klansmen: Guardians of Liberty

BY

Bishop Alma White, A. M.

Author of "The Story of My Life" (4 vols.), "The
New Testament Church" (2 vols.), "The Ku Klux
Klan in Prophecy," etc. (See back of book); and
Editor of "The Good Citizen."

ILLUSTRATED BY

Rev. Branford Clarke

PRICE, 50c, POSTPAID

THE GOOD CITIZEN

Zarephath,

1926

New Jersey

INTRODUCTION

By Arthur H. Bell,

Grand Dragon, Realm of New Jersey,
Knights of the Ku Klux Klan.

HAVING had the honor of reading the advanced copy of Bishop Alma White's latest book, *Klansmen: Guardians of Liberty*, which in truth may be termed a sequel to her masterpiece, *The Ku Klux Klan in Prophecy*, it is with a great deal of personal satisfaction that I offer my few words of recommendation and approval in the form of an introduction.

The author of this book, Bishop Alma White, from my personal knowledge has a great ambition to bring forth to the public the true program which the Roman Catholic Hierarchy has developed to consummate its ambitious desire, and it is my conviction that through her books, especially this one you now hold, her life purpose shall be fulfilled.

The power of desire is far reaching. Frequently one finds some reference to that ideal state of mind in which one is free from all desire. It is not a condition that appeals to the author of the book, the writer of this introduction, or the membership of the Klans of the Nation, nor can it be upheld by the student of man and his history. It is desire—the manifold, out-reaching needs and wishes of men—that has been responsible for the great things done on this earth. The human race without desire would become stagnant and get nowhere—in fact would become a race doomed to perish for the very lack of a desire to live. The man or woman who desires nothing will in turn get nothing, do nothing, and be nothing.

Bishop White in this volume will unfold to the

reader the desire of the Roman Catholic hierarchy to control the minds of men and to take from them their own desire of liberty and freedom. She will also unfold the desire of the Klan to forever safeguard the liberty of individuals and to allow the human race its God-given right to develop itself in every way for the best interests of mankind, a desire free from the shackles of heathen, pagan dogma, that will bring forth greater benefits for humanity.

Whipped and stung by fierce desire, men have builded empires, and with the rise and fall of such empires they have gone on and on developing civilization and adding ever to the equipment of life. The Roman Catholic Hierarchy has a great desire to build an empire, an empire to kill liberty and to place in shackles the human race to serve in blind submission and eventually to die under the ambitious plans of an intolerant, liberty-hating creed. The Knights of the Ku Klux Klan and their allies have also a great desire to build an empire, an empire of liberty and love, in place of submission and hate, an empire in which men and women will freely serve one another in following out the teachings of Christ and the principles of Christian America.

Bishop White has rightly named the Klansmen, "Guardians of Liberty," and to the readers of this book she will undoubtedly prove the Roman Catholic Hierarchy's right to the name, "Assassins of Liberty."

Read, my friends, and learn the truth; then in your knowledge go forth and spread the truths of this book throughout the Nation and create a desire. To desire is—to live, and Protestant America must live to save the world.

CONTENTS

Notice to the Reader

As in my former book, **The Ku Klux Klan in Prophecy,** so in this, the various chapters are taken from lectures delivered at different times and places, therefore they have little if any connection one with another. Each chapter stands alone and is complete in itself. It has been my effort in each to show the ambitions of the Roman Catholic hierarchy, and to make clear the great principles for which the Knights of the Ku Klux Klan are contending. There will be found some repetitions, which could not be avoided in a work of this character, but these repetitions will in no wise detract from the value of the book.

May the great principles of freedom for which our forefathers contended be preserved by the patriots of this generation, is my earnest prayer.

The Author.

CHAPTER I

The Hebrew Rock

MATTHEW 16:13-23

Peter was the recognized leader and spokesman of the apostles and stood for the Hebrew race. Jesus directed His conversation to him when He wished to teach His disciples and others great truths concerning His own Messiahship. He said, "Whom do men say that I the Son of man am? And they said, Some say that thou art John the Baptist: some, Elias; and others, Jeremias, or one of the prophets. He saith unto them, But whom say ye that I am? And Simon Peter answered and said, Thou art the Christ, the Son of the living God. And Jesus answered and said unto him, Blessed art thou, Simon Bar-jona [son of Jonah]: for flesh and blood hath not revealed it unto thee, but my Father which is in heaven." This truth had not only been personally revealed to Peter, but as the representative of the children of Abraham it had come down through the prophecies of which the Hebrews had been the

7

THE ROCK UPON WHICH THE TRUE CHURCH IS BUILT

custodians, as God had been dealing with them and not with the Gentiles. The revelation of His Son through Moses and the prophets had not been given to the Gentiles, neither was it to come from this source.

"And I say also unto thee, That thou art Peter [*Petros, rock*], and upon this rock I will build my church; and the gates of hell shall not prevail against it." Jesus meant that His Church was to be built upon the Hebrew rock which designated His own origin and proved His right to the throne of this world,—a question that would sooner or later be disputed. In this dispute the Romish Church was destined to take the lead in trying to rival Christ by putting the Pope, their so-called infallible head, on the throne of the world.

The stock of Abraham had to be brought into the foreground to forestall the possibility of the Gentiles taking to themselves and appropriating the promises of Israel as Rome has done. It has been the mammoth scheme of Satan down the ages, to supplant Israel and to turn the kingdom over to the Pope and the devil.

Peter's life and disposition did not indicate

that he was the most spiritual one among the disciples and that in this sense he merited any special favors. There are no grounds for the claim of Roman Catholics that the Church was built upon this disciple. This erroneous teaching has deluded and enslaved millions down the ages. As the head of the disciples Peter acknowledged Christ's Messiahship, but he showed at times great stupidity and ignorance. When Christ tried to show him how He must suffer and be offered up on Calvary, Peter said, "Be it far from thee, Lord: this shall not be unto thee." His lack of spiritual discernment and a real conception of Christ's mission on earth caused him to receive a severe rebuke. Jesus said, "Get thee behind me, Satan: for thou art an offense [scandal] unto me: for thou savourest not the things that be of God, but those that be of men." This rebuke was aimed at apostate Israel who did not know their Messiah. They wanted their king to be crowned then and there. They did not wish to be humiliated by His death on the cross as the Scriptures had foretold. Peter, expressing the general sentiment of apostate Israel, said, "Be it far from thee,

Lord: this shall not be unto thee." They were tired of the Roman rulers, and wanted a king of their own.

The Jews are everywhere a separate and distinct people, living apart from the great Gentile masses, as they did in Egypt. They have maintained their own peculiar characteristics, regardless of the powers that have operated against them and sought their destruction, and will continue to do so until the world's redemption has been completed and the kingdom of Christ has been set up on the earth. The lineage of Him who shall sit on David's throne can be traced back through forty-two generations, and consequently His right to the throne is indisputable.

The Hebrew race was not broken at the time of the dispersion, nor has it been since. Have the plans of Omnipotence failed? To every enlightened mind the truth remains that the triumph of the ages through God's chosen people is yet to come.

Did Jesus make a mistake when He said, "And I will give unto thee [the Church built on the Hebrew rock] the keys of the kingdom of heaven: and whatsoever thou shalt bind on earth shall be bound in heaven, and whatsoever thou shalt loose on earth shall be loosed in heaven"? The Church against which the gates of hell shall not prevail originated with the Jews and must be perpetuated through Christ their king, and not the Pope. Therefore the papacy has no grounds on which to base its claims as being the only true Church and that the Italian Pope, the so-called successor of St. Peter, is the infallible head and ruler of the world.

He who sits at the right hand of God holds the keys and will vindicate Himself and defeat all the demon-possessed agencies that have tried to rival Him since the fall of Lucifer. The Scriptures say that God visited the Gentiles "to take out of them a people for His name" (Acts 15:14). Paul was recognized as the great apostle to the Gentiles to begin this work. It is enough for the Gentiles to have the honor of being members of the Bride of Christ. But to claim to be the root, branch, and trunk of the tree, and all that is involved, is to supplant God's ancient people and transfer the glory of Israel to the Gentiles who constitute the wild olive branch that was grafted into

HOLY BIBLE

PETER'S PENCE

CONFESSIONAL

TEMPORAL POWER

CHRIST OR THE POPE

WHICH WILL YOU CHOOSE?

the good olive tree (Romans 11).   Roman
Catholics, who claim that the true Church is
built upon Peter, must go down in humiliation
and everlasting defeat as will all others who
would rival Christ in the rulership of this
world.

Daniel said, "I beheld till the thrones were
cast down, and the Ancient of days did sit,
whose garment was white as snow,....and,
behold, one like the Son of man came with the
clouds of heaven, and came to the Ancient of
days, and they brought him near before him.
And there was given him dominion, and glory,
and a kingdom, that all people, nations, and
languages, should serve him: his dominion is
an everlasting dominion, which shall not pass
away, and his kingdom that which shall not
be destroyed" (Daniel 7:9-14).

Notwithstanding the spiritual desolation of
Israel, God's hand has been upon them in all
of their sojournings among the nations, and
through them He will get great glory to His
name. The fact that the Hebrews have held
together is a guarantee of this and that a remnant will yet be established in the land of their
fathers, preparatory to the coming of Christ,

who will appear on Mount Olivet with His Gentile Bride to rule the world in righteousness.

The Jews today are away from home, away from the land that God said should be theirs forever. A remnant, at least, must return to their own country and accept their long-rejected Messiah. To prevent calamity God's plans must be carried out and this cannot be done until the sons of Jacob are nationalized in Palestine.

One of the signs of the times is the drift of the higher institutions of learning and the Protestant churches away from orthodoxy. Decadence in spiritual life and morals in the past few years has been so rapid as to astound the civilized world, but nevertheless it is the fulfilment of prophecy in the winding up of the Gentile age. When the cup of iniquity has been filled divine wrath can no longer be restrained, and calamity will fall.

The trend of woman's fashions, the profligacy, crime, and immorality everywhere, show the nakedness of the Church and are tokens of the judgments of God that are soon to fall upon the nations.

Pagan Rome has multiplied her sorceries

and deceived the people of this and other generations for fiifteen hundred years, and a climax has been reached. The bold headlines of the Romanized press that do the "Scarlet Mother" reverence forbode calamity. There are those, however, who are making a protest against her aggression. They compose the white-robed army in the United States who, if faithful, will continue to find favor with God and lead the hosts on to greater achievements and victory. Since the Lord saw fit to place Klansmen in the breach for Protestantism there has been a new reformation and no doubt judgments have been deferred. In the days of Nineveh impending calamity was stayed for a period of one hundred and fifty years when the people repented under the preaching of Jonah.

The Invisible Empire is now placing the stones and repairing the wall where enemies of the Cross and our civil liberties have well-nigh wrecked it.

10   **There is Hope in the Cross.**

ALMA WHITE.   ARTHUR K. WHITE.

1. There is hope, bless - ed hope, In the old rug - ged cross, When its
2. There is hope, bless - ed hope, In the old rug - ged cross, When the
3. There is hope, bless - ed hope, When your all is re - signed And the

glo - ries e - ter - nal you know; If you car - ry it through And to
toils of this life are all o'er; If His name you a - dore, And His
grac - es of Christ 'fill your soul; On the wings of His love He will

CHORUS.

God you are true, Re - joic - ing in Him you will go.
love you im - plore, With Him you shall dwell ev - er - more.   There is hope, bless - ed
bear you a - bove, Where a - ges e - ter - nal shall roll.

hope In the old rug-ged cross, There is hope in its life - giv-ing stream; At the

rit.

foot of the cross, Counting all for Him loss, The Sav - ior your soul will re - deem.

Copyright, 1925, by Pillar of Fire, Zarephath, N. J.

From "The Silver Trumpet," Published by Pillar of Fire.

What Saith the Word of God?

For I am not ashamed of the gospel of Christ: for it is the power of God unto salvation to every one that believeth; to the Jew first, and also to the Greek.

Romans 1:16.

————

But God forbid that I should glory, save in the cross of our Lord Jesus Christ, by whom the world is crucified unto me, and I unto the world.

Galatians 6:14.

————

Finally, brethren, whatsoever things are true, whatsoever things are honest, whatsoever things are just, whatsoever things pure, whatsoever things are lovely, whatsoever things are of good report; if there be any virtue, and if there be any praise, think on these things.

Philippians 4:8.

————

We then that are strong ought to bear the infirmities of the weak, and not to please ourselves.

Let every one of us please his neighbor for his good to edification.

For even Christ pleased not himself; but, as it is written, The reproaches of them that reproached thee fell on me.   Romans 15:1-3.

————

Therefore we ought to give the more earnest heed to the things which we have heard, lest at any time we should let them slip.   Hebrews 2:1.

CHAPTER II

Rome's Claims without Scriptural Foundation

The Roman hierarchy claims the Catholic Church has survived the wreck and ruin of the ages and is the pillar and ground of truth. Age and decay are twin sisters,— where one is found you will find the other. The Church that is true in one age may not be found faithful in another. The seven churches described by John in the Book of Revelation, with two exceptions, were wholly or in part in a state of apostasy before the end of the first century. So, beware of the cruel Old Mother, who has fed the flames of martyrdom with her victims, and who has put millions to death in the name of her so-called holy religion.

She has added one strange and un-scriptural tenet after another to her gigantic system of greed and graft, and has done more to corrupt the world than all other known agencies. History shows that a Church once fallen has never reformed, but

19

as the years have passed has gone from bad to worse. But out of the wreck and ruin of those that go down, God has always raised up new movements to represent His cause and to give light to the world. They have come to us since the fall of the Apostolic Church under different names; and have always suffered persecution. Rome has always persecuted true Christians, or those who constituted the visible body of Christ. Her deluded and unscrupulous masses know practically nothing of the Bible or of what it teaches. They hold to the traditions of men, rather than to the Word of God. They worship dead saints, deify and invoke the Virgin Mary, knowing nothing of Christ and His great salvation. Jesus is almost always pictured by them as being in the arms of Mary, thus minifying His power in the eyes of the people, while the Virgin takes the place that He should have in their hearts.

Roman Catholicism is paganism, and cannot be called Christian in any sense. The worship of the Virgin Mary sprang from the old pagan custom of worshiping some goddess. Many of Rome's forms and ceremonies have been adapted from paganism. Where can you

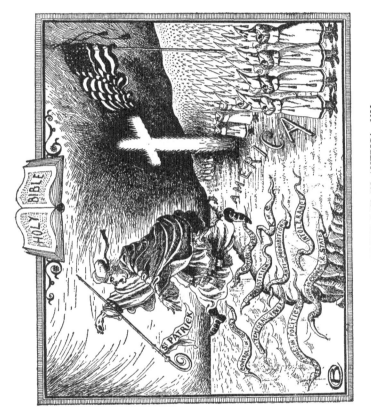

ST. PATRICK'S DAY IN AMERICA—1926

find a Roman Catholic clergyman who knows
anything about the new birth, of which Christ
told Nicodemus? Where a priest has been
truly converted his eyes were opened to
the idolatrous system to which he belonged.
The Scriptures clearly teach that all idol-
aters have their place in the lake of fire
(Rev. 21:8). It will take more than ceremonies, vain repetitions, and external applica-
tions of water to save men from their sins.
What they need is the Gospel preached in its
old-time purity and power, without any priestly
embargo upon it.

"Go ye into all the world and preach the
gospel to every creature." What has this kind
of preaching to do with the traditions of men
and their heathen philosophies? This command
was given to humble laymen and others from
the lower walks of life, who perhaps had never
seen the inside of a college, much less had received degrees. The true Gospel is the power
of God unto salvation to everyone that believes; in other words, every person who meets
conditions will receive Christ and become a
member of the true Church, the invisible or
spiritual body composed of all true believers.

This is not the old religio-political machine controlled by the Roman hierarchy, thirsting for world dominion and willing to pay any price to obtain it. Since democracy is founded upon the principles of Christianity, the true Church is democratic, and is the very opposite of Rome with her autocracy and so-called infallibility. In the annals of history there has never existed a more autocratic system than Roman Catholicism.

Love and mercy should characterize all of one's relationships with one's fellow man. Christianity is the only religion that has divine love, the principle so much needed in the world today. Love will change the attitude of men's hearts toward one another, and there is none of it in the Roman Catholic creed. Autocracy is another name for the "Scarlet Mother," with all of her wealth and display.

The Pope claims to be the Pontifex Maximus, the supreme head of all worship, the vice-gerent of God on earth, and yet there is not one word of scripture in support of this assumption.

The multitudes will yet break their shackles and rise above this pagan religion,

MR. FACING-BOTH-WAYS

masking under the sign of the Cross.   The
light of the Gospel is destined to radiate to the
ends of the earth and disperse the darkness of
superstition and bigotry. The Christian Church,
the Ku Klux Klan, and other Protestant
agencies are now at work to bring it about.

In Mexico and South America, where
Roman Catholicism has rested like a nightmare upon the people for centuries, a new
day is dawning. Here ignorance and
superstition are giving place to Christian enlightenment.

Mexico is struggling for her very existence as a nation. Bishop James Cannon, Jr., of the Methodist Episcopal Church South, has been in Mexico for the past eight years supervising the work of that Church. He says:

"For 350 years the Mexican people lived under the practically unrestrained domination of Roman Catholicism. That Church had it within its power to write the history of Mexico as it would, and in fact did write it. The Church had the opportunity to show what it could do with a good native stock in a country with unlimited natural resources. It could have taught the Indians to read and write; to build comfortable, clean, sanitary houses; it could have preached the gospel of truth, honesty, chastity, and set an example of high moral Christian conduct; it could have developed a 'civil society, cultured and adorned with all the arts of civilization.'

"It did none of these things.

"It did build great and beautiful cathedrals and lavish millions of money on the decoration of them and upon the shrines, images, altars, and vestments therein. It did multiply costly churches throughout the country, in some sections one for each great estate. It did develop over one thousand parishes with over twenty thousand ecclesiastics, over two hundred and fifty convents and monasteries, with over eight thousand inmates vowed to celibacy, over one hundred and fifty missions, and eighteen male and twenty female orders. It did accumulate a vast amount of property, so that at the time of Juarez in 1857 it was conservatively estimated that the Church controlled over one-third of the material assets of the country, lands, houses, mortgages, and so forth. It did interfere continually, arrogantly, influentially and disastrously in the political affairs of the nation. The Church did manifest great activity and power in these things."

A former official of the Mexican Education Department says, in substance, that slavery prevailed for centuries in Mexico, the people being used as beasts of burden. They were branded with hot irons like cattle, were maltreated, exploited, and killed by a people who claimed they were making the country safe for civilization. The center of life of the communities was the Church, which controlled all the activities of the people. They were forced to erect temples in every village and to contribute for their enrichment and magnificent ornamentation. The Church got control of most of the gold and silver, which went to Rome and to Spain,—$27,000,000 of gold in one year having been transported to the Old World, and $3,000,000,000 worth of silver and other metals in three centuries. The Church exacted ten per cent of the products of the land. "The ground had to be blessed by a priest

before sowing, processions and religious services were organized to pray for rain in times
of drought." People were kept under control
of the Church from birth to death, and even
after they were dead. There was "mass in the
morning, the rosary in the evening, confession,
communion, extreme unction, the benedic-
tion of the grave within a Church cemetery,
and responsories for the departed," domestic
animals had to be taken to church once a year
to be blessed, etc., [all of which had to be paid
for]. "The priest was pastor, physician, chief
of police, school teacher, and judge."

"Only fifty years after Mexico City was occupied
by Cortes, the infamous tribunal of the Holy Inquisition was established in Mexico. Luis Gonzales
Obregon, in *Mexico Viejo* (Old Mexico) writes: 'From
that day terror began among the good inhabitants..
..Fear swept over all....No one lived at ease; secret
denunciation threatened every one; unfortunate was he
who gave grounds for the least suspicion, and unhappy
was he who merely neglected to wear a rosary.' In
one day alone, on April 11, 1649, 107 persons were
burned alive or tortured to death by the Inquisition
in Mexico, most of them simply because they were
accused of professing the Jewish religion."

In regard to education this former
official states that "during all these years

(350) of almost absolute rule,....only
the dominant aristocracy learned to read and
write." He also says that the Roman Catholic
Church has opposed woman suffrage, prohibition, and labor organization. It has excom-
municated persons who participated in land
subdivision, and young men who attended the
Y. M. C. A., and "at the end of nearly four

UNCLE SAM: "WE DON'T NEED YOU IN THE U. S."

centuries of control by the Church 90 per cent
of the Mexicans did not know how to read or
write.   Yet the so-called Church now professes
sympathy for the poor Mexicans who ask:
"Who is going to teach and educate us if the
priests and the nuns do not?' "

President Calles of Mexico is quoted as having
said recently regarding the priests:

"They think that everyone should conform to their
dogmas.   At present they cannot do as they used to
do.   They cannot persecute individuals or members of
other religions.   The Mexican government had to
punish them and to suppress the outrages of Catholics.

"The Catholic clergy has always been attempting
to keep from obeying the laws.   They have never been
willing to obey any authority, except that of Rome.
The Catholic clergy has never been a factor in the de-
velopment or uplifting of the nation.   There also has
been a tendency to keep political power in their hands.
The Catholic clergy cannot longer prevent the great
movement for the reform of social and economic conditions in Mexico.   This is the origin of the difficulties
we have had in Mexico, with the   Roman   Catholic
clergy."

For four centuries the people of Mexico
have been ground down under the heel of Roman oppression.   While this is not a matter
in which the United States Government can
interfere, yet every patriotic man and woman

should give Mexico all the moral support possible.

Everywhere Rome has operated she has held the people in gross ignorance, and however unjust and unreasonble, she has used force to establish her claims. She has never hesitated to shed the blood of those who have opposed her in her assumption of power. She has been the Inquisitor of the ages. How can people with any reasonble knowledge of her present and past history accept her dogmas and bow at her idolatrous shrines?

CHAPTER III

Shall Rome Have the Next President?

Who the next president of the United States shall be, is a question for every lover of liberty to help to decide. It is evident that Rome is marshalling her hosts and enlisting the powers of earth and perdition to defeat the Prohibition and Protestant causes in America by sending Al Smith, the papal Governor of New York, to the White House. Since he was defeated by the K. K. K. for the nomination on the Democratic ticket in 1924, every agency of the Pope, in this and the Old World, is being used to put him through in the next presidential campaign.

Tammany Hall, with its notorious history of corruption, greed, and graft, heads the list, followed by the George E. Brennan machine of Chicago, and their counterparts in all the great centers of the United States. During the latter part of 1925 Governor Smith, on a visit to Chicago, called at the throne room of

"IT'S A LONG, LONG WAY TO THE WHITE HOUSE"

Cardinal Mundelein and stayed an hour and a half. The German cardinal is a member of the Pope's college and lives in a mansion which contains perhaps a hundred rooms. When the foreign cardinals invaded the United States in June (1926) Governor Smith, together with the papal Mayor of New York City, gave them a public reception at the Municipal Building. And then, during the great show at Chicago, Smith was on hand, ostensibly to worship the pancake god, but in reality to further his prospects for the Presidency. It is reported that the Governor of the great State of New York knelt and kissed the hand of the Pope's representative.

Will the good people of America permit such a calamity to fall upon this republic, as the election of a papal president, after all its marvelous history?

Since America has been a nation, there has never been a Roman Catholic president to manipulate the reins of government in behalf of the Roman Pontiff. If Smith should be eleced president then the goal for which the Vatican strives would be in view. Free speech, free press, free public schools, etc., would soon be things of the past.

The bootleggers, the moonshiners, the great liquor interests, and law-breakers of every class and kind, are now operating in behalf of the Smith candidacy.

His repeal of the Mullan-Gage Enforcement Act, and the consequent encouragement of the bootleggers, brewers, and other law-breakers all over the country, are sufficient to reveal his character and what might be expected if he became president. History repeats itself. When the reins of government are placed in the hands of wicked men, calamity is not far distant. "When the righteous are in authority, the people rejoice: but when the wicked beareth rule, the people mourn" (Prov. 29:2).

Read the story of the massacre of St. Bartholomew, or of the work of the Duke of Alva in the Netherlands, or of the persecutions of Bloody Mary, if you have any disposition to encourage Rome's political leadership in this day and age.

Fellow citizens! shall we sleep while the weasel of intrigue and corruption cuts the

HIS MASTER'S VOICE

throat of liberty and turns the government over to the Pope and his inquisitors? How long can these lecherous vampires masking under the sign of the Cross deceive an enlightened people? The Knights of the Ku Klux Klan have been a mighty force to thwart the plans of the hierarchy and to disillusion the public.

In the eleventh century, it was decided by Hildebrand—Gregory VII—that instead of kings and emperors crowning popes, the popes should crown the kings and should themselves have the supreme dictatorship of the world. As the centuries have come and gone this Satanic ambition has not abated, but is stronger today than when the Inquisition was in full force.

Al Smith will never be the President of the United States if those who hate Rome's iniquitous system will exercise their prerogative in blocking his way. But how to stir up the Christian churches and the unsuspecting Protestants who hold the balance of power, is the all-absorbing question. See to it that none but Americans are placed on guard.

Komics

TOOK THE HINT IN REVERSE

A countryman came to Boston to visit some relatives and to see the sights. He remained until patience on the part of his hosts, a married couple, ceased to be a virtue.

"Don't you think, my dear fellow," remarked the husband one day, "that your wife and children must miss you?"

"Hadn't thought of that," was the calm reply. "Thanks for the suggestion; I'll send for them."—*Boston Transcript.*

———————

During the World War a doughboy whose gun had become shattered by an exploding shell became panic stricken and started running towards the rear. After he had gone some ten miles at a record pace an officer commanded him to halt.

"Here, don't you know that there's a big battle going on up at the front?" said the officer. "What do you mean by running away like this when you should be up there doing your bit?"

"Y-y-yes, I-I-I know there's a big battle on up there," stuttered the breathless and trembling doughboy.

"Then what are you doing way back here?" demanded the officer.

"I-I-I'm just spreading the news, sir," said the infantryman.

"Spreading the news," scoffed the officer. "Well, I think you are a coward and I'm going to have you court-martialed and shot at sunrise tomorrow.

"By the way," he added, "do you know who I am?"

"N-n-no," said the doughboy, "I don't know who you are, sir."

"Well, I'm your general," said the officer.

"Am I that far back?" exclaimed the doughboy, and fainted from exhaustion.

BOSSES WERE WISE

The heads of a big manufacturing plant had this notice posted at the beginning of the summer season:

New Rule for Our Employees

All requests for leave of absence on account of toothache, severe colds, and minor physical ailments, and on account of church picnics, weddings and funerals and the like, must be handed in to the foreman in charge of your department before 10 a. m., on the morning of the game.—*Houston.*

CHAPTER IV

The Price of Liberty

Liberty has been purchased at a great price and our safety depends upon eternal vigilance. Millions have enjoyed the blessings that have come through the sacrifices of others, but only a few are willing to suffer that these achievements may be maintained.

The Declaration of Independence was the greatest blow to tyranny that the world had ever known. After a heated discussion on the 3d of July the document was unanimously adopted on the 4th. When the hand of the sexton grasped the rope of the old Liberty Bell in Carpenter's Hall, Philadelphia, on that memorable day, the world was seized with convulsions destined to shake tyrants from their thrones. A year later (June 14, 1777) the Stars and Stripes were unfurled to the breeze. Betsy Ross made the flag from strips of a white shirt, a blue jacket, and some red flannel. The great principles for which the

RINGING THE LIBERTY BELL

colonists stood gave the flag distinction over all other national colors.

On July 2, 1788, twelve years after the signing of the Declaration of Independence and five years after the treaty of peace between the Colonies and Great Britain had been ratified, the Congress of the new nation was notified that nine states (a sufficient number) had voted approval of the Constitution, and the new government was set in motion on a day in the following March which happened to be the 4th. This date has since remained as the initial one for the President and for Congress.

The Constitution, based on the New Testament, is the greatest document that was ever framed by mortal mind. Its principles are as undying as God himself. One hundred thirty-eight years of national prosperity have furnished ample proof of this assertion. Shall we let the proud achievements of our forefathers go down in ignominy and shame?

These two great documents, sacred to every true American, must hold their own against all odds if we are to continue a free and unfettered people. The birthpangs of a new nation gave us both of these wonderful instruments of freedom. They came to us as a heritage from our forefathers who laid down their lives on the altar of their country that we might enjoy the peaceable fruits of their sacrifice. Shall all be lost, or shall we rise to the occasion and contend for the faith of our fathers? Shall any flag be floated in "the land of the free and the home of the brave" except the Stars and Stripes? God forbid!

To secure religious freedom was the chief object of those who gladly suffered and sacrificed all in the early history of our country. Heroes and heroines of the Cross did not hesitate to launch out on a perilous sea to risk their lives among the American savages, rather than continue in bondage to the old monarchical systems that had made life so intolerable for them. Privation and hardship characterized every step they took. They did not come to America as mere sightseers or adventurers; they came to establish principles that would liberate the human race from the tyranny of the Old World.

Is there a person with a drop of patriotic blood in his veins who can think of the sacri-

fices made at Bunker Hill, at Valley Forge, in
the crossing of the Delaware at Trenton, or in
the winter at Morristown without being moved
to the depths of his being? There were those
who deserted at the time they were most
needed, as has always been the case where it
has cost so much to be true, but the memory
of the sturdy heroes who stood at their posts
of duty until Cornwallis surrendered to their
Chief, will live in the hearts of true Americans until the end of time.

Many of the soldiers had devoted wives
and mothers living in extreme poverty as the
result of the demands the war had made upon
them. There were vacant chairs at the family board; husbands, sons, and brothers were
absent, some of whom would never return.
How these loved ones longed to hear familiar
steps and voices! But alas! too often their
happy dreams of reunion were never realized.
The greatest sacrifice that can be made is that
which touches the home and its relationships,
and under such conditions the truest patriotism and devotion are awakened in the breast.

We need more than a display of the national
colors, and such demonstrations as character-

ize our 4th of July celebrations. There must
be a real infusion of patriotic blood into the
veins of our people. The rising generation,
that has never had the opportunity to learn in
the school of adversity, should be taught to
appreciate the principles of free government.

How prone humanity is to forget! What
changes a few years have wrought! It took
the World War to awaken people to the nation's peril. The historians, no doubt, have
done what they could to keep fresh in the
minds of the rising generation the sacrifices
of others; but to say that there has been
great stupidity and lack of appreciation and
true patriotism on the part of the people is to
put it mildly. It is everywhere manifest
that the enemies of free government are worm-
ing their way into the Capitol at Washington
with the one object of changing our customs
and laws and ruling with a rod of iron. There
has been little concerted action to offset the
propaganda of the foes within our gates. Our
ports have been wide open to aliens of every
caste and creed. Millions have come to our
shores from the slums of lower Europe, holding fast their allegiance to a foreign poten-

tate (the Pope of Rome), and among these are some of the worst of criminals.

Three of our Presidents have been shot down by men who were brought up in the Roman Catholic Church. Two of these assassins were foreign born. Why should we shelter those who would kill our rulers and sink our nation to the level of their own depravity and degradation?

Rome is the arch foe of liberty. Her system is a misfit in the United States and can never be made to harmonize with the principles of free government.

When George Washington took the oath as our first President he stooped and kissed the Bible; and no person with any less devotion to its pages and principles has the right to aspire to follow in his footsteps and be President of these United States. And this includes both the Old and New Testaments. Rome would take the Bible, not only out of our public schools, but from our homes and churches, and substitute her paganistic creed with its worship of the Virgin Mary, dead saints, images, bones, and other relics. Her lust for power is everywhere manifest in the

THE PROTECTING HAND OF TRUE AMERICANISM

politics of the country, and when once the reins of government are taken out of the hands of Protestant rulers our doom is sealed.

Upon the President of the United States hinges the welfare of one hundred and twenty millions of people. His responsibility staggers the imagination. But Rome will usurp this office unless there is concerted action on the part of all true Protestants. Should she succeed, a reign of intolerance would be instituted such as never has been known in the civilized world. There is no time to lose in combating the un-American forces that are determined to wrench the government from the hands of Protestants and make it subserve the purposes of the Vatican. Shall the Italian Pope, through his cardinals or others, dictate our policies and command our army and navy? This is the burning question for every lover of liberty to consider.

———

Komics

Mr. Blimp: Remember, the hand that rocks the cradle rules the world. Don't forget that, dear.

Mrs. Blimp: Then you come right in and rule the world a while. I'm tired.—*Good Hardware.*

Komics

HOW FRANKLIN GOT A JOB

It is recorded of Benjamin Franklin that when as a poor boy he asked for work at a printer's in London, the foreman, doubting whether an American could do anything well, asked if he could really set up type.

Franklin stepped at once to a case and set up John 1:46: "And Nathanael said unto him, Can there any good thing come out of Nazareth? Philip saith unto him, Come and see."

This was done so quickly and accurately and conveyed such a delicate reproof, that he obtained employment at once and was rapidly promoted.—*Kind Words.*

———

The young lady was very gushing about her love of books. The professor of literature to whom she was speaking, however, was rather skeptical as to the extent of her knowledge. "Of course you know Sir Walter Scott's works," he gently inquired. "I do; I do!" she cried, ecstatically. "His *Lady of the Lake,* most wondrous of books, you have read that?" "Yes, indeed," was the eager response, "I simple adore it." "And Scott's *Marmion,* and *Kenilworth,* and *Peveril of the Peak?*" he continued. "Yes, yes," she joyfully avowed. "Scott's Emulsion, too?" he inquired, enthusiastically. "That," she cried, "is the very best he ever wrote."—*Methodist Recorder.*

CHAPTER V

Klansmen of the Revolution

Many people today, like blind Samson grinding in the mill of the Philistines, are unable to trace the origin of the Knights of the Ku Klux Klan back to the early settlers of our country, whose spirit and principles have been brought down from Revolutionary times to the present day. Since the first efforts were made by the colonists to throw off the yoke of tyranny placed upon their necks by George III, 100 per cent Americans have been the most conspicuous characters in our history. The Stamp Act produced great provocation and they resisted it.

"Taxation without representation," said the immortal James Otis, "is tyranny." Otis held the position of Advocate General for the colonies, but resigned that office in order to attack the King's Writs of Assistance.

Samuel Adams, "The Father of the Revo-

lution," was a member of the Assembly in the
Massachusetts legislature. It was said that he
had the most "radical love" of liberty of any
member of that body. Adams denounced the
proposed Stamp Act at a meeting held in Fan-
euil Hall, the "Cradle of Liberty." But in spite
of all the protests that were made, Parliament
passed the law in 1765. The result was that
delegates—100 per cent Americans—from nine
of the colonies met in New York in the Stamp
Act Congress of 1765. Here was drawn up a
Declaration of Rights which said: "(1) The
American Colonies possess the same rights as
all other British subjects; (2) but they are not
represented in the English Parliament; therefore Parliament has no right to tax them."
When the hated stamps came, the people destroyed them, and even the boys—Junior Klansmen—shouted, "Liberty, property, and no
stamps!" Many leading citizens pledged themselves to buy no more English goods until the
Stamp Act was repealed.

So great was the protest on the part of the
100 per centers that the Stamp Act was repealed in 1766. But its repeal was followed by the imposition of taxes upon

BURNING THE STAMPS IN THE STREET

window-glass, paper, paints, and tea. These articles Parliament thought the colonists could not do without. The king wanted money to pay his soldiers who were sent here to keep the colonists in subjection; also to pay the governors, judges, and other officials of the Crown, the object being to keep the colonists entirely dependent upon the King and ready to do his will. This was called the Townshend Act. Great was the indignation aroused among the Colonial Klansmen, who thereupon refused to import any of the taxed articles. There were some, like Samuel Adams, who said they would eat, drink, or wear nothing imported until all the duties on these goods should be taken off. The patriots declared that they would not take the tea brought to them, even as a gift.

But the cargoes of tea continued to arrive at New York, Boston, Philadelphia, Annapolis, and Charleston. In only one instance, however, that of Charleston, was the vessel allowed to discharge the tea, and then it was left on the wharf to spoil. At Philadelphia the captains of the vessels were told that if they did not turn back they would be tarred and feathered. At New York the Sons of Liberty took action equally decided. At Annapolis the captain of the tea ship was compelled to burn his vessel, tea and all.

The case that caused the most excitement occurred at Boston. Three tea ships came into the harbor, but the patriots refused to allow the cargoes to be unloaded. The Governor in turn refused to let the ships go back to England unless they were unloaded, so the Klansmen, under the leadership of Samuel Adams, made up their minds to do the unloading in their own way. A great Klavern was held in the Old South Meeting House to determine what could be done. That night a band of citizens in full *REGALIA* rushed down to the wharf and emptied every chest of tea, nearly $100,000 worth, into the harbor. A Bostonian asked, "Will tea mix with salt water?" The patriots settled that matter and the tax at the same time.

General Gage with his soldiers was now in full control of Boston. Samuel Adams was keeping the colonists informed by letters, of all that was going on and preparing them for united action. In 1774 the Continental Congress was held in Carpenter's Hall, Philadel-

THE BOSTON TEA PARTY

phia, to decide what should be done. George Washington, a "Master Mason," was one of the delegates. Everybody wanted peace if it could be had with justice. At this congress a Declaration of Rights was issued, demanding the right to levy all taxes. The King was humbly petitioned to redress their wrongs; but as has been said, they might as well have petitioned the Great Stone Face in the White Mountains of New Hampshire.   •

Massachusetts, in 1775, set up a government independent of the military rule of General Gage. It was headed by John Hancock, an influential merchant of Boston. The colonists then raised twelve thousand volunteers. The spirit of liberty was universal. A patriotic publication in South Carolina said, "One soul animates three millions of brave Americans," though they were scattered over a territory two thousand miles long. But the Carolina paper forgot the Tories, who constituted a third of the population. These hyphenates and pacifists refused to take up arms against the King. They believed the quarrel could be settled without firing a gun or drawing a sword. In the end the Tories—those who opposed the

100 per cent Americans—were driven out of the country and others seized their houses and lands.

General Gage, at Boston, sent his soldiers to Concord, twenty miles away, to destroy powder and provisions stored there by the patriots. His soldiers also had orders to go by Lexington and arrest Samuel Adams and John Hancock, who were stopping in that city. It was published by the papers in London that the heads of these two men would soon be brought and displayed there.

The British troops waited until just before midnight, April 18, 1775, to start on their campaign of plunder and murder. But Paul Revere, the noted Colonel of the Klavaliers of Boston, was on guard. At his request two lanterns flashed their signal from the steeple of the Old North Church, and the gallant Klavalier galloped away through the country to give the alarm. He was soon at Lexington and at the gate of the house where Samuel Adams and John Hancock were asleep. A guard cried out, "Don't make so much noise!" "Noise!" shouted the brave man, "you will have noise enough before long. The regulars

PAUL REVERE'S RIDE

are coming!" And true to his word, just before day on the morning of the 19th, a company of General Gage's soldiers under Pitcairn
marched on to the village green, where a number of minute-men had gathered.

"Disperse, ye rebels!" ordered Pitcairn,
but not a person moved. Then the command
was given to fire, and seven of our Colonial
Klansmen fell dead.

At the Concord bridge the Red Coats were
met by our patriots. It was the opening battle
of the Revolution. Here the first British were
killed and the first British graves were dug.
The regulars then drew back, leaving the
Americans in possession of the bridge, and began their march toward Boston. The march
became a retreat, something like a run.

At Lexington they were met by Lord
Percy with reinforcements. Here the British
soldiers dropped panting on the ground with
their tongues out. The minute-men had chased
them all the way to Charlestown. Three hundred Red Coats lay dead or dying on the
ground. They had marched gaily out of Boston to the tune of Yankee Doodle, played in
ridicule of the Americans, but when they re-

entered the town they had had quite enough
of all that was Yankee for that day. The
next morning the British found themselves
shut up in Boston and the siege began.

To the thoughtful mind the leaving of
Concord bridge in the hands of the Americans
had much significance. For more than
two hundred years the Americans had been
trying to build a bridge across the dark gulf of
ignorance and superstition, from the old monarchical systems of Europe to the New World
of liberty and democracy. Thenceforth, as a
result of their heroism, new religious and
political standards were to be raised on the
Western Hemisphere,—standards to which all
the world was sooner or later to come.

The Americans, amid great privations and
suffering, had built a bridge and were destined
at all odds to hold it.

The Revolutionary War covered a period
of nearly seven years, from the time the first
battle was fought at Concord on the morning
of April 19, 1775 until Oct. 19, 1781, when
Cornwallis surrendered at Yorktown. After
the close of the war an imperfect government
was in operation for another seven years, or

until Washington took the oath as the first president of the United States. Then was the Constitution in full force.

The parallel between the Klansmen of the Revolution and those of today is obvious to anyone who has eyes to see. Though the opposing forces have shifted and changed in name and nature, the issues of today are just as vital and will be as far-reaching in their consequences as were those of the Revolutionary War.

———

Komics

A school teacher said to her class of boys:

"I am going to give you each three buttons. You must think of the first as representing Life, the second Liberty, and the third Happiness. In three days I want you to produce these buttons, when I shall expect you to tell me what they stand for."

On the appointed day she asked one of the boys for his buttons.

"I ain't got 'em all," he said. "Here's Life, and here's Liberty, but mother has gone and sewed Happiness on my trousers."

———

Tailor (having measured customer for suit)—And how would you like the pockets, sir?

Scott—Weel—just a bit deefficult to get at.

Komics

THE BOOK NO GOOD TO HIM

Hiram Diggs writes thus to the *Tranction Bulletin*: "I received the book you sent me, which is named 'What Makes the Gasoline Engine go.' I ain't read it yet, because what's the use reading it when I don't care what makes the gasoline engine go as long as it goes, which mine don't only occasionally. What I want to know is, 'What Makes the Gasoline Engine Stop?' If you got a book entitled that, send me one. I want to know what makes my gasoline engine stop when everything is O. K. and nothing is the matter."
—*Selected.*

SYNCHRONOUS WOBBLING

Not long ago, in a certain university city, a lady was crossing a street when she saw a bicyclist approaching. She stopped, then dodged backwards, and as the rider had swerved in order to pass behind her there was a collision, and both had a fall, though neither was much damaged.

"If you hadn't wobbled, sir," said the lady angrily, as he helped her to rise, "this wouldn't have happened."

"Neither would if it have happened, madam," he replied, "if you hadn't wobbled, or if you had wobbled in a contrary direction from my wobble. It was our concurrent and synchronous wobbling, so to speak, that caused it."

Then the cyclist doffed his cap, mounted his bicycle and wobbled on.—*Pearson's Weekly.*

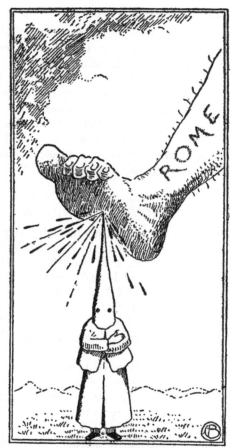

WATCH YOUR STEP

CHAPTER VI

A Great Crisis Coming

That a great crisis is coming to the nation, no one with spiritual discernment can doubt. The Scriptures show that we are living in the time of the most astounding fulfilment of prophecy of the ages. Great political and religious issues are now in the forefront and the wheels of time are moving toward their rapid conclusion. But as yet our churchmen and statesmen have been dealing with these things in the abstract and usually with gloved hands, —so few daring to make bare the real facts for fear of the loss of position, or other consequences that might interfere with their own personal ambitions.

When this nation was founded, men and women were willing to sacrifice their reputations, their property and their lives to uphold the principles of righteousness. But it is seldom, if ever, that a person can be found now who aspires to leadership who would say with

Henry Clay, "I would rather be right than President." Nearly every office-seeker who had a ghost of a chance to ascend a throne, so to speak, and wield a scepter in the political realm, has a little world of personal ambition of his own to consider that outweighs the interests of the general public. What could be more alarming or portentous of calamity than for such people to hold the reins of power?

Is it not time to ring the alarm bells and prepare for the on-coming conflict so vividly foretold by John in the seventeenth and eighteenth chapters of Revelation? It will be too late for weak and unsophisticated Protestants to make amends when the terrors of God's wrath are sweeping the earth for the crimes of the "Harlot Mother."

Note the following:

"The Catholic Church has the right and duty to kill heretics because it is by fire and sword that heresy can be extirpated. Mere excommunication is derided by heretics. If they are imprisoned or exiled they corrupt others. The only recourse is to put them to death. Repentance cannot be allowed to save them, just as repentance is not allowed to save civil criminals. For the highest good of the Church is the unity of faith, and this cannot be preserved unless

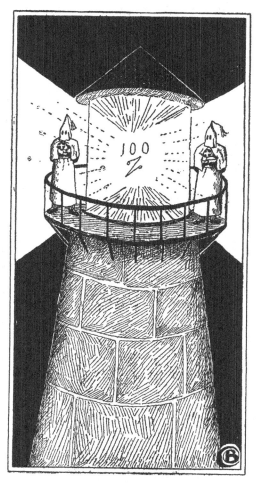

ON THE WATCH TOWER

heretics are put to death."—Prof. Hugh O'Donnell (Irish Catholic), author of *The Ruin of Education in Ireland*.

Oh, for an awakening of the national conscience that has so long slept, in the face of the fact that the enemies of freedom have well-nigh accomplished their purpose in taking from us our God-given heritage.

The modern churches are almost out of the fight. They have made so many concessions to foreign propagandists in national and religious affairs that they have ceased to be vital factors in the hands of an all-wise God to thresh down the mountains of iniquity and stop the rivers of blood. We must now look to unexpected sources for true men and women who, like Elijah, will take the heads off the false prophets and bring an end to selfish interests and corruption in both church and state. According to the Scriptures it will take another war to do it, which will be a time of trouble such as never was from the beginning of the world, and "except those days should be shortened, there should no flesh be saved" (Matthew 24:22).

The following quotations from Roman

Catholic sources show the attitude of Rome toward our government.

"I expect to see America classed as a Catholic nation. . . We exhort all Catholics to devote careful attention to public matters and take part in all municipal affairs and elections, and all public services, meetings and gatherings. . . Furthermore, it is generally fitting and salutary that Catholics should extend their efforts beyond this restrictive sphere and give their attention to national politics."—Encyclical of Pope Leo XIII.

"How near at hand do you think is the time when America will be dominantly Catholic? Things move with rapid strides these days, and the recent creation of three American cardinals has brought the Church once more to the forefront."—The *Catholic Missionary Union.*

"Many non-Catholics fear us as a political organization and are afraid that the Catholic Church will dominate and rule. We are working quietly, seriously, and I may say, effectively."—*The Missionary*, 1909.

Archbishop Ireland is quoted as saying:

"We can have the United States in ten years, and I want to give you three points for your consideration: the Indians, the negroes and the common schools."

The younger generation of this nation should review and study United States history with new zeal and inspiration, taking into consideration the sacrifices of men who willingly laid down their lives for the principles upon which the government was founded.

James Monroe, the fifth President of the United States, was responsible for what is known as the American Doctrine or the Monroe Doctrine. He advocated our isolation from Europe, expressing the sentiment that had grown up among the people forbidding entanglements with foreign alliances and European interference in American affairs. There should be no European colonization on the Western Hemisphere, and any attempt to extend Old World systems on American soil would be dangerous to our peace and safety.

But what are conditions as they exist today? The fact is, the Monroe Doctrine has been violated, but with such subtlety, under a cloak of loyalty, as to deceive the very elect. We have millions of foreigners in our great cities, living according to their European customs, controlling the markets and the elections, and manipulating the money power of the country. They have changed our laws and customs to suit their purposes just as truly as if they had taken down the Stars and Stripes and hoisted other emblems. The "Scarlet Mother" with her great religio-political machine has the cooperation of the sons of Israel in these matters and is working out her schemes to make America Catholic. She has openly declared that should she get in power,

"What the church has done, what she has expressly or tacitly approved in the past, that is exactly what she will do, expressly or tacitly approve in the future, if the same circumstances occur."—*Bronson's Review.*

So, fellow citizens, you may know by this what to expect when Rome succeeds in getting command of our army and navy. If such a calamity should befall this nation it will be too late to repent of the stupidity, and often utter indifference, of Protestants.

The subtlety with which Rome is conspiring against our public school system is one of the strongest arguments that we are skirting along the edge of the precipice. Our school books are being revised to suit the program of the Catholic Church, who says:

"The American school system is a national fraud, a social cancer presaging the death of national morality."—*Catholic Telegram.*

THE SUBTLE CONSPIRATOR

"We persist in our attitude of dissatisfaction with the public schools. They are quite as unacceptable to us as they ever were."—Sermon by Archbishop Dowling.

"The law of the Church in this diocese debars from the sacraments parents who send their children to public schools."—Bishop Foley.

"The Church question in America is a school question, in other words, its fate tomorrow depends upon its state today. If throughout the states children of Catholic parents were schooled in a Catholic atmosphere, and under Catholic teachers, in another generation Catholics would be on top."
—Father Vaughn.

"We don't want to be taxed for Protestant or Godless schools. Let the public school system go to where it came from—the devil."—*Freeman's Journal* (Catholic) New York.

"Education does not lie within the scope of civil authority, wherefore the State cannot, without violating higher and holier rights, usurp the right and discharge the duty of educating the young."—Rev. James Conway in "The Right of Our Little Ones."

WHO HAS BEEN INTO THAT JAM?

CHAPTER VII

Faith of Our Fathers

If the people of this generation do not take up the work of our forefathers and fortify themselves against exploitation by foreign foes, inevitable doom is written upon our escutcheon. The only way to preserve our heritage is to carry on the work that they so heroically began. In this pleasure- and money-loving age, it will take real faith and courage to do this.

Our numbers have multiplied until we now have more than a hundred and twenty millions of people who claim allegiance to the Stars and Stripes. Yet it is a deplorable fact that not all of this number by any means can be counted on as loyal subjects. There are millions in the United States who have sworn allegiance to another flag who may be properly designated "hyphenated" Americans. It may be difficult to secure a Gideon's band, but the number can be had, and as truly as the Midianites were routed by the cry, "The sword of the Lord and of Gideon," the victory can be won by One Hundred Per Cent Americans.

The great feats recorded in earthly warfare have never been accomplished by numbers. The Psalmist said, "Some trust in chariots, and some in horses: but we will remember the name of the Lord our God." The all-important thing is to know that we are enlisted in a righteous cause, and to have the support of Him who said, "Five of you shall chase an hundred, and a hundred of you shall put ten thousand to flight" (Lev. 26:8).

Since the Revolutionary Fathers gained national independence our western border has been extended from the Ohio River to the Pacific coast and our population has increased from less than four millions to thirty times that number. The great difficulty now is the danger of sinking by the weight of numbers. There must be a winnowing process to sift out the chaff. People have had to be proved in all ages, so will they have to be proved now in order to hold the fortresses.

Pure religion and patriotism are unselfish, and we must have both to succeed. Our forefathers had spiritual vision and kept their gar-

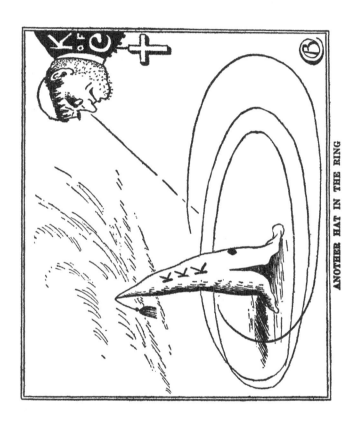

ANOTHER HAT IN THE RING

ments unsullied until the work committed to
their hands was accomplished and others took
their places. True devotion and sacrifice characterized the efforts that they put forth in behalf of freedom. The people were ready for
the thundering tones of the old Liberty Bell
and knew the moment of every stroke of the
hammer. There were tremendous issues before them that would mean a life and death
struggle in their efforts to throw off the yoke
of tyranny, but they had counted the cost and
expected to suffer the consequences. To show
they were not in the dark as to what would
follow they took down at this time a leaden
statue of George III in New York, melted it
up and made it into bullets.

The hardships that the Colonists had en-
dured and the injustice they had suffered at
the hands of the half-mad and tyrannical king
of England put steel into their characters,
and they were not to be trifled with. They had
been in a school of experience, where lessons
had been learned that enabled them to lay the
foundation of a great republic. The struggle
for existence in an unbroken wilderness had
made them self-reliant and resourceful.

When the Declaration of Independence was signed it had been nearly 150 years since the Pilgrim Fathers landed at Plymouth seeking a place where they could work out their own destiny and worship God according to the dictates of their consciences.

There were now thirteen colonies under the control of the British crown. The Colonists could easily have chosen the path of least resistance, but the fires of liberty were burning in their breasts, and the treatment they had received only fanned the flames. Nothing daunted, they continued with the true pioneer spirit to overcome their difficulties and their foes. The result was they planted the banner of liberty on the heights of victory and wrote their names high on the walls of fame.

The Revolutionary Fathers did not want peace that was not honorably obtained. Too well they knew it would be short-lived, and it was loathsome and repulsive to them. The keynote sounded by Patrick Henry at the Virginia Convention fired every heart and caused decisive action to be taken after the British had closed the port of Boston. This noted orator and patriot said: "There is no longer any room for hope. We must fight. I repeat it, sirs: we must fight."

There was no other course to pursue that would have had a feather's weight with the British government. William Pitt and Edmund Burke were making eloquent speeches in Parliament in favor of America. The action then taken by the Colonists proved the strength of their arguments. Burke said if they tried to tax the Americans they would have as hard a time as did the farmer who tried to shear a wolf instead of a sheep.

For many years our gates were kept wide open. We asked nothing as to the health, character, or intentions of those who came to our shores. We simply said, "Come in," shook hands with them and told them to make themselves at home. In other words:

"Come on, come on, make no delay,
Come from every nation, come from every way;
Our lands they are broad enough, there's cause for no
    alarm,
For Uncle Sam is rich enough to give us all a farm."

By the beginning of the twentieth century

THE WOLF IN SHEEP'S CLOTHING

twenty millions of them had arrived. This
number was largely composed of Poles, Rus-
sian Jews, Italians, and others from lower Europe. It could not be otherwise than that many
of them would sow the seeds of discord and
the harvest would have to be reaped sooner
or later. Among them were Socialists, Anar-

chists, and those opposed to all forms of stable government. In recent years, before our restrictive immigration laws were passed, they came at the rate of more than a mililon a year. With this great, seething mass of humanity, fomenting trouble, what will the outcome be, if Americans fail to keep the upper hand in governmental affairs? But it is not too late if the right methods are used.

Pure Americanism has nothing in common with Romanism, Socialism, and Communism. The aims and purposes of those belonging to the first group are to Romanize America and bring it into subjection to the iron-clad, medieval, liberty-destroying autocracy of a vain, pompous, corrupt ecclesiasticism. Their purpose is to make the Roman Pontiff the dictator of American destinies. The purpose of the last group is to *internationalize* America and to destroy its social and political history. To this class belong the Pacifists, those who are calling for a reduction of armaments and the destruction of our national defense. Among them may be some who have good intentions, but are kept in the dark as to the real intents and purposes of those who would destroy all military training in our schools and colleges, with the plea that this would settle the question of there ever being another war. The foreign propagandists who are heading such movements have their headquarters in Russia, and would abolish all patriotic traditions and sentiment, junk the navy, and disband the army. Their determination is to reduce all people to the same social and economic level, and advocate any means whatsoever for the accomplishing of this, from mere legislation and political revolution to a reign of terror.

The sentiment of an unenlightened public is, Can there be any cause for alarm, since we have had 150 years of glorious history and have proved ourselves equal to every emergency without or within our borders? But such optimism is extremely dangerous at this time, when without a doubt we are up to a national crisis, and men and women of the purest American blood will be needed to meet the issues.

The laxity of enforcing the Prohibition liquor laws is undermining our existence as a sovereign power. Constitutional government is breaking under the strain of lawlessness and crime caused by the great influx from the Old

World, of immigrants who have no respect for our laws. The Revolutionary fathers had a vision comprehensive enough to see this danger, and hence originated the Monroe doctrine, which is as truly being violated as if there were the outright seizure of territory and colonization.

Job said, "The thing which I greatly feared is come upon me, and that which I was afraid of is come unto me" (Job 3:10). It now appears that the thing most dreaded by the early patriots has come, and how to avert greater calamity is the problem to be solved. It is evident that if the country is saved it will have to be done by the Bible and the ballot, or by bullets. The latter by all means should be the last resort.

We have awakened to the fact that the great majority of immigrants have come to our shores to profit by the sacrifices made by others, and, having had no part in them, their interests have been almost wholly selfish. Where the melting-pot has failed to do its work, these immigrants are found in groups, standing for the despotism of the old-line, Dark-Age monarchy, or that of wild, unbridled anarchy.

WHAT SAITH THE WORD OF GOD?

Hear, O Israel: The Lord our God is one Lord.

And thou shalt love the Lord thy God with all thine heart, and with all thy soul, and with all thy might.

And these words, which I command thee this day, shall be in thine heart:

And thou shalt teach them diligently unto thy children, and shalt talk of them when thou sittest in thine house, and when thou walkest by the way, and when thou liest down, and when thou risest up.

And thou shalt bind them for a sign upon thine hand, and they shall be frontlets between thine eyes.

And thou shalt write them upon the posts of thy house, and on thy gates.

And it shall be, when the Lord thy God shall have brought thee into the land which he sware unto thy fathers, to Abraham, to Isaac, and to Jacob, to give thee great and goodly cities, which thou buildedst not,

And houses full of good things, which thou filledst not, and wells digged, which thou diggedst not, vineyards and olive trees, which thou plantedst not; when thou shalt have eaten and be full;

Then beware lest thou forget the Lord, which brought thee forth out of the land of Egypt, from the house of bondage.   Deut. 6:4-12.

———————

For he established a testimony in Jacob, and appointed a law in Israel, which he commanded our fathers, that they should make them known to their children:

That the generation to come might know them,

even the children which should be born; who should arise and declare them unto their children:

That they might set their hope in God, and not forget the works of God, but keep his commandments.

Psalm 78:5-6.

———————

Whosoever shall seek to save his life shall lose it; and whosover shall lose his life shall preserve it.

Luke 17:33.

———————

Stand fast therefore in the liberty wherewith Christ hath made us free, and be not entangled again with the yoke of bondage.   Galatians 5:1.

———————

But the end of all things is at hand: be ye therefore sober, and watch unto prayer.   1 Peter 4:7.

CHAPTER VIII

Shall Church and State Be United?

Rome seeks to unite church and state and rule the world through her papal head. When she fails in this aspiration her old paganistic system will totally collapse. If the Ku Klux Klan is true to its great principles it will spell the doom of Romanism. Jesuitical deception and secret diplomacy are being exposed by the Klan in its dissemination of light and truth.

Pope Pius IX is quoted as saying,

"We have taken this principle for a basis: that the Catholic religion with all its rites ought to be exclusively dominant, in such sort that every other worship shall be banished and interdicted. It is a cause of supreme bitterness to the heart of the Holy Father not to be able otherwise to impose a limit to so much evil, as he certainly would if he could make use of other means to bridle their insane license."

The old "Harlot Mother" in recent years has faced defeat in many places where she has heretofore suceeded in wielding the scepter of power. There is no source of greater ignorance and superstition than is embodied in the old ecclesiaticism with its idolatrous shrines and the worship of the Virgin Mary, yet Priest Hecker is quoted as saying,

"Ere long there will be a state religion in the United States and that state religion is to be the Roman Catholic."

Pagan Rome is our most dangerous liability. The masses are trained to do the bidding of the hierarchy, and there is no crime too great for them to commit. They are taught that "the end justifies the means."

The Western Watchman, St. Louis, Dec. 24, 1908, is quoted as follows:

"Protestants were persecuted by France and Spain with the full approval of the Church. The Church has persecuted. Only a tyro in Church history will deny that. When she thinks it good to use physical force she will use it. The Catholic Church gives no bonds for her good behavior."

The public has been too long in a state of gullibility concerning Rome's secret activities. The old deceiver has worn the mask down the ages and what sometimes appears to be true and virtuous is simply an outward covering. The so-called Houses of the Good Shepherd, or slave-pens, and the charitable activities of the K. of C. carry with them suspicion everywhere, and people should know the whole truth concerning them. During the World War divine retribution was visited on the European countries that were dominated by the Pope; and greater judgments are yet to come.

Some of the teachings of Rome follow:

"The Pope has the right to annul state laws, treat-

ON GUARD

ies, constitutions, etc.; to absolve from obedience thereto, as soon as they seem detrimental to the rights of the Church, or those of the clergy.

————

"It would be very erroneous to draw the conclusion that in America is to be sought the type of the most desirable status of the Church, or that it would be universally lawful or expedient for State and Church to be, as in America, dissevered and divorced."
—Encyclical of Pope Leo XIII.

The present monarchical systems of Europe all have the framework of Romanism. Knock the frame down and the old system will go to pieces. Who knows this any better than the hierarchy?

During the great struggle, when hundreds of thousands of our young men were making the supreme sacrifice, the Roman Catholic clergy in southern Ireland were inciting demonstrations against conscription, while Protestant Ulster heroically stood with the Allies in behalf of civilization. Men of every nationality in the United States were called to the colors, but there was no law to draft an alien Irishman, who was a loyal subject of the Pope who found shelter under the Stars and Stripes. In the meantime England protected Ireland from the fate of Belgium, France, Poland, etc. Italy bore her part in the great struggle, and other smaller nations did what they could, but what did stalwart Irishmen do while the death struggle was going on?

The New York *Times,* of April 7, 1918, said,

"The inclusion of Ireland in the area of conscription, contingent though it be, has had precisely the effect foretold by Englishmen who tried to prevent it. Both the Catholic hierarchy and the Nationalist Party have been driven into the arms of the Sinn Feiners and it is improbable that they will be able to escape from the embrace for many days. The majority of Irishmen are not at all concerned about their representative principle and their essential point of view was unmistakably expressed to me by a gentleman of whom I inquired whether he would accept conscription from a home rule party. "To h— with home rule. If a Dublin Parliament means conscription we would rather live under Westminster rule forever.'

"The bishops and the clergy go with the Pope, and the people are only too eager to go in such a direction with the bishops and clergy. The outrage to representative principle is only an excuse and the result would have been the same if the Dublin Parliament would have enacted conscription unanimously."

The above clearly shows the attitude of the Roman hierarchy in Ireland where the clergy had sufficient numbers and power to

A COME-BACK HE WAS NOT EXPECTING

withstand the Government. Is not this in keeping with their policy and teachings?

Note the following as samples of Rome's teachings:

"It is necessary that one sword should be under another, and that temporal authority should be subject to the spiritual power.... Moreover, we declare, say, define, and pronounce it to be altogether necessary to salvation that every human creature should be subject to the Roman pontiff."—*Canon Laws.*

And the *Catholic World*, July, 1870, is quoted as saying,

"If the Pope's authority and that of any civil government come into conflict upon any vital point, the Catholic is to act in the nineteenth century precisely as he did in the first, second, and third centuries.

The boast of the K. of C. in this country as to having done so much to win the war carries but little weight where Roman Catholic principles and policies are clearly understood. Both Roman Catholics and Protestants were drafted and they had to go or suffer the consequences, and now Rome boasts of the loyalty of her sons to the Government, when, as all know, it was a question of compulsion.

Let our great American organization continue to radiate light and truth, and a new and better civilization will be built up on the wreck and ruin of the old papal system. There is naught that can stay the progress of this new reformation. Our white-robed army is determined to thwart the plans of the old hierarchy to rob us of our God given heritage.

———

DOES THIS SOUND LIKE AMERICANISM?

The following questions and answers are taken from a *Manual of Christian Doctrine*, twelfth edition, published by J. J McVey, Philadelphia, Pa., which bears the imprimatur, Patritius Johannes, Archiepiscopus Philadelphia. (August 10th, 1909). Used as text-book in Roman Catholic High Schools.

Page 132—Question 115. "In what order or respect is the State subordinate to the Church?

In the spiritual order and in all things referring to that order."

Question 116. "What right has the Pope in virtue of this supremacy?

The right to annul those laws or acts of government that would injure the salvation of souls or attack the natural rights of citizens."

Question 117. "What more should the State do than respect the rights and the liberty of the Church?

The State should also aid, protect, and defend the Church."

Question 119. "What then is the principal obligation of heads of States?

Their principal obligation is to practice the Catholic religion themselves, and, as they are in power, to protect and defend it."

Question 120. "Has the State the right and the duty to proscribe schism or heresy?

Yes, it has the right and the duty to do so both for the good of the nation, and that of the faithful themselves; for religious unity is the principal foundation of social unity."

Question 122. "May the State separate itself from the Church?

No, because it may not withdraw from the supreme rule of Christ."

Question 124. "Why is liberalism to be condemned?

1—Because it denies all subordination of the State to the Church; 2—because it confounds liberty with right; 3—because it despises the social dominion of Christ, and rejects the benefits derived therefrom."

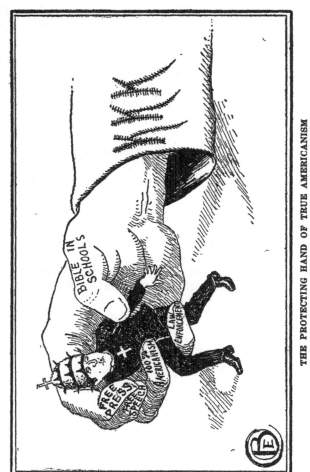

THE PROTECTING HAND OF TRUE AMERICANISM

CHAPTER IX

Dangers Threatening the Nation

Law enforcement should now be the all-absorbing theme of every lover of liberty. Laxity in enforcing the Prohibition laws is not only menacing constitutional government, but our very existence as a sovereign power. This may seem to be exaggerated to those who do not know the facts and are not concerned about finding them out.

The Eighteenth Amendment was the result of a long-fought battle covering a period of more than a hundred years in the United States. Thirty-two states had voted dry before the national Prohibition law was passed. Now, to close our eyes to the dangers we are facing, and to sleep while a criminal minority reverse the wheels of progress by the modification of the Volstead act, would be the tragedy of the ages. This would eventually lead to the open saloon as every sensible person knows.

The thought of such a thing staggers the

THE MODERN SAMSON IN DESPERATE STRUGGLE WITH THE BEAST OF DRINK

imagination and produces a sort of creeping paralysis. But we must throw off any state of lethargy and summon all our powers to defeat the foes of liberty.

The American home has had a breathing spell from the nightmare of the liquor curse by a few years of actual experience, and no argument produced by the enemies of Prohibition can change the minds of the millions who have been benefited thereby. They will not agree to another legalized program to make criminals under the despotism of strong drink. No word of tongue or pen has ever been able to depict the tyranny of alcohol. Neither can the imagination grasp what it would mean to undo that which has been accomplished at so great a cost and throw this nation back under the lash of the old oppressor.

Shall America, which now has the proud distinction of setting a noble example for the whole world, go back and grovel in the dust of imbecility and inefficiency, to be scoffed at and made a byword? God forbid! Think what it would mean to permit the old "parasite" to come in again and tie the hands of those

who operate the machinery of this great republic, and bring about the collapse of all our
achievements. And yet we have men in our
legislative halls who have taken the oath to support the Constitution of the United States and
who claim to have the welfare of the people at
heart, who are laying under contribution all
the powers of perdition to bring back the open
saloon.

But "the die is cast and the book written"
against alcoholic poison. Prohibition stands
out today as the crowning victory of this nation. We have set our stakes and will not be
robbed of our heritage by intriguing, corrupt
politicians who would deluge the world with
the liquid fire for monetary and selfish interests. The minds and hearts of our people have
been enlightened, and they will not be enthralled
again. We are not ready to be bound and
gagged and made to subserve the purpose of the
Vatican.

The great offensive is now on to break down
democracy and to place a dictator in the White
House. The first step to this end is to bring
back the liquor curse, the strong ally of the
Pope and the commercial men of the Old

World. Foreign propagandists contending for liquor would place the reins of government in the hands of the so-called god-man on the banks of the Tiber and make him the dictator of earth, heaven, and hell.

The greatest blow that the old religio-political machine ever received was when the Prohibition Amendment was placed upon our statute books. But, true to form, the "Scarlet Mother" (Rev. 17:16) never gives up the fight until compelled to do so.

The ballot in the United States has done its work, and if the law is not enforced, revolution is as sure to follow as night follows day. An unshackled and enlightened people will never tolerate a repetition of the old saloon days.

The scripture says that the wicked shall be turned into hell and all the nations that forget God (Psalm 9:17). This includes the drunkards and those who contend and vote for liquor. God's word says, "Woe unto him that giveth his neighbor drink, that puttest thy bottle to him, and makest him drunken also" (Habakkuk 2:15). Plagues written in the book of Revelation may be expected to follow any re-

BOON COMPANIONS

vision of our prohibition law that would give greater license to its enemies.

Revelation 8:10-11 is a direct prophecy concerning liquor and its woful consequences. It shows how the waters were turned bitter, causing the death of many. The sun was then darkened. What could bring greater darkness than to forfeit the ground we now hold? If ever men and women of sterling qualities were needed it is now. Shall we send "wet" legislators to Congress to undo the Eighteenth Amendment?

The clergy for the most part have become impotent and it remains for the laity to rise up in protest against the program of foreigners who would rule and ruin the nation. Law-enforcement must be the watchword of every person who would not become an ally to the powers that would turn back the wheels of progress and enslave the human race.

The liquor men and the owners of vice dens profit by the election of men to office who espouse the cause of the "wets." The men who own the breweries and the gambling dens are up to all the tricks of the trade. Among them are those who operate the white slave dens and traffic in innocent girls. What better ally could the Pope have in the United States than these?

———

WHAT SAITH THE WORD OF GOD?

Every man that striveth for the mastery is temperate in all things.   1 Cor. 9:25.

———

And be not drunk with wine, wherein is excess, but be filled with the Spirit.   Ephesians 5:18.

———

Be not among winebibbers; among riotous eaters of flesh;

For the drunkard and the glutton shall come to poverty: and drowsiness shall clothe a man with rags.

Who hath woe? who hath sorrow? who hath contentions? who hath babblings? who hath wounds without cause? who hath redness of eyes?

They that tarry long at the wine; they that go to seek mixed wine.

Look not thou upon the wine when it is red, when it giveth his colour in the cup, when it moveth itself aright.

At the last it biteth like a serpent and stingeth like an adder.   Proverbs 23:20-21; 29-32.

———

I beseech you therefore, brethren, by the mercies of God, that ye present your bodies a living sacrifice, holy, acceptable unto God, which is your reasonable service.

THE DEFENDER OF THE 18TH AMENDMENT

And be not conformed to this world: but be ye transformed by the renewing of your mind, that ye may prove what is that good, and acceptable, and perfect will of God.

For I say, through the grace given unto me, to every man that is among you, not to think of himself more highly than he ought to think; but to think soberly, according as God hath dealt to every man the measure of faith.

For as we are many members in one body, and all members have not the same office:

So we, being many, are one body in Christ, and every one members one of another.

Having then gifts differing according to the grace that is given to us, whether prophecy, let us prophesy according to the proportion of faith;

Or ministry, let us wait on our ministering; or he that teacheth, on teaching;

Or he that exhorteth, on exhortation: he that giveth, let him do it with simplicity; he that ruleth, with diligence; he that sheweth mercy, with cheerfulness.

Let love be without dissimulation. Abhor that which is evil; cleave to that which is good.

Be kindly affectioned one to another with brotherly love; in honour preferring one another;

Not slothful in business; fervent in spirit; serving the Lord;

Rejoicing in hope; patient in tribulation; continuing instant in prayer;

Distributing to the necessity of saints; given to hospitality.   Romans 12:1-13.

CHAPTER X

The Little Red Schoolhouse

On a recent automobile trip from New Jersey to Colorado and return, the author had ample opportunity to observe the condition of the public schoolhouses and their lack of necessary conveniences and outside equipment. Colorado was the only state where modern facilities for the comfort of the children seemed to be provided. In some other states there were no walks around the buildings, and the children were wading through the mud as best they could on roads approaching the schoolhouses and on the play-grounds. The buildings on the outside were unspeakably unsanitary; and in some instances the stables where the horses were kept to take the children back and forth to school were in a dilipidated condition. Sometimes cheap automobiles were to be seen standing near a school, but no place had been provided for their protection.

In Nebraska, Iowa, Illinois, Indiana, Ohio

and Pennsylvania the schoolhouses and outside equipment were found to be twenty-five to fifty years behind the times. In some of the buildings it would be impossible for the children to keep warm in cold weather as there was nothing between the ground and the floors to keep the wind out. The homes near these schools were often modern structures, up to date in every way. One can readily see how parents living in such homes are often induced to send their children to parochial schools, and why Rome is making such a desperate fight to discredit our public schools and to prevent any appropriation of money for their upkeep and advancement.

There has never been a single plausible reason why the bill which provides for an educational department in the cabinet should not be passed. There is nothing more apparent than that those who oppose such a measure are un-American and working in the interests of a foreign potentate.

An enemy to the public school is an enemy to the Constitution. We are thankful that a white-robed army has arisen, a mighty host that will put the Bible in the schoolroom and forbid the lecherous hand of popery to inter-

THE BIBLE MUST BE PLACED IN EVERY SCHOOLROOM

fere with our free institutions. May God hasten the day when the conscience of the nation will be aroused and speedy action taken.

Komics

The teachers at a certain school try to make the papers as up-to-date and interesting as possible. During a recent examination one of the questions read thus: "If one horse can run a mile in a minute and a half and another is able to do the same distance in two minutes, how far ahead would the first horse be if the two ran a race of two miles at these respective speeds?

One pupil returned his paper with the query. unanswered, except that he had written on the sheet: "I refuse to have anything to do with horse-racing."
—*Stillson Zenith.*

George Washington was very small and very new to the life of the public school. "And so your name is George Washington?" said the teacher.

"Yessum, Jorge Washin'ton."

"And I suppose you try to be as nearly like him as a little boy can, don't you?"

"Lak who, ma'am?"

"Like George Washington."

The youngster looked puzzled. "Ah kain't help bein' lak Jorge Washin'ton," he replied stoutly, "cose that's who ah am."—*Ohio State Journal.*

CHAPTER XI

Autocracy vs. Democracy

No Romanist can consistently claim to believe in democracy, since it is opposed to every cardinal principle upon which the papacy is founded. Consistency is rarely found in the ranks of the Pope's followers who work under cover, while concealing their real purpose.

The "Old Mother" has been rightly termed "The Great Deceiver"; she has played her part in the history of other countries and her plans must be thwarted in the United States.

The liberty for which our forefathers fought, and sacrificed all they possessed, is not the heritage of the Woman on the back of the beast (Rev. 17) who would rob us of our Constitutional rights and all that life holds dear.

One can readily see what the ultimate end would be, and what abuses would be inflicted upon the people of this nation should the "land of the free and the home of the brave," fall into the hands of Romanists. To awaken an unsuspecting public and prepare it for the oncoming conflict is now our great responsibility.

The greater portion of our citizenry are leaving political affairs largely to machine bosses, whose hands are full of bribes and whose consciences are seared as with a hot iron. One needs to go back only a little more than half a century to see how the gulf has widened between the men who stood for principles, and those who manipulate the forces of evil and enlist them in behalf of the elevation of wicked men.

There is not a doubt that we are skirting along a precipice and that the old roads are everywhere giving way.

We needed a revival of patriotism, and it has been brought about through the efforts of the Knights of the Ku Klux Klan, to the astonishment of the whole country and of the world. The younger generation have had but little knowledge of American History from the fact that Rome has had the audacity to tam-

AUTOCRACY DOES NOT SUIT UNCLE SAM

per with our text-books, thus keeping them
in darkness. There has also been a lack
of interest on the part of parents, teachers,
and others, in trying to impress upon the minds
of youths what it cost in sacrifice and blood
to build a great republic. They should know

something of the political issues for at least a
hundred and fifty years back and what the enemies of freedom did to tie the hands of the
law-makers, which finally resulted in two great
wars with England, and later that of the Civil
War, which caused the loss of a million lives
and crippled the progress of half of our population for more than sixty years.

The subject of States' Rights has been a
bone of contention since Revolutionary times.
The Federalists believed in a strong central
government.   To this class belonged John
Adams, the second president, and his immortal son, John Quincy Adams, the sixth president, both of Massachusetts.   And to this class
also belonged, in a more moderate form, James
Madison of Virginia, the fourth president of
the United States.

The people, more especially in the Southern States, who had suffered under the
tyranny of the old European monarchies,
were determined not to be caught in what they
feared was the steel-trap of Federalism, advocated usually by Northern statesmen. They
were afraid that if a strong central government were built they would find themselves in

a worse predicament than they had been in before they fought to throw off the yoke of European oppression. It took these two great political factions to keep the young republic from going on the rocks. There had to be men of great minds and unbreakable characters, who would stand for principle when the batteries of the enemy turned loose shot and shell upon them. Some such men are found in the catalog of our presidents, and others were the greatest and most efficient judges and generals the country has ever produced.

The United States has an infinite store of wealth in the lives of her great men, with which there has been no parallel in history. This is the legacy of freedom dearly bought; people born, not as the children of chance or some special fortune through the royal lines of ancestry, but as those who by wisdom, industry, and sacrifice have made their own fortunes and written their names on the walls of fame to be examples to the unborn generations. In a great republic almost anyone can get out of life what he is willing to put into it. It is good fortune for any person to be well-born. Blood cannot be altogether ignored in the building of character; but the opportunities offered to those whose forebears have been unknown, means that a crown of glory awaits them if they persevere where there is an open door in a country like ours.

There is no other place where democracy has been tried out as it has been in the United States and where equal opportunities are offered to all. Shall the increasing of our numbers, our facilities, and our great national wealth cause us to forget the pit whence we were dug? And shall we submit the most important things concerning our peace and happiness to those who are operating a great religio-political machine with the avowed purpose of making America Catholic and placing the reins of government in the hands of the Italian Pope?

Note the following:

"The Pope has given the order to make America Catholic. . . The first step in the making will be the election of one of the American cardinals to the Papacy, the removal of St. Peter's to Washington. Cardinal Gibbons [published before Cardinal Gibbons' death] to be president and every non-Catholic will be driven out of the army and navy."

—*Catholic Sun.*

THE CAPITOL IS STILL IN THE HANDS OF AMERICANS

"Ere long there will be a state religion in the United States, and that state religion is to be the Roman Catholic."—Priest Hecker.

"The Pope has the right to give countries and nations which are non-Catholic to Catholic regents who can reduce them to slavery."

Roman Catholic Canon Law.

The old political machine is largely controlled by intriguing belligerents who at heart have no real love for our flag. This is the condition in which we now find ourselves, with dead-falls and traps set everywhere for unsuspecting Protestants.

New York is dominated by Tammany Hall, the most corrupt political machine in the history of the country, carrying out the program of the "Scarlet Mother." Most Roman Catholics belong to the Democratic Party, regardless of the fact that the Pope is the greatest autocrat the world has ever known. In the history of the world no ruler or pretender has ever compared with him or laid claim to the power which he assumes the right to exercise. But it has ever been the policy of the "Scarlet Mother" to change her color like the chameleon and to adopt any measure as a means to the end for which she strives. And so it is in the case of the politics of New York. Al Smith and his political backers have had much to say in favor of States' Rights, and the fact is the doctrine of States' Rights, if made effectual would destroy the whole papal system. But with the subtlety that has always been her characteristic, Rome uses it in her efforts to secure world dominion. At heart Smith does not believe in States' Rights. If true to his religion he is a staunch opponent of all forms of government by the people. If the hierarchy should gain the ascendency in this country they would destroy all the Bibles, set the Pope on the throne at Washington, and use the army and navy to help execute his will. How long will a just God forbear? Shall political Rome continue to blind the masses and hold them in bondage to the world's greatest autocrat? Thank God for those who would die rather than cower before the enemies of freedom, and sell their birthright to the man on the Tiber.

THE SIGN THAT BROUGHT AN AVALANCHE

Komics

Jake was a worthless and improvident fellow. One day he said to the local grocer: "I gotta have a sack o' flour; I'm all out, an' my family starvin'."

"All right, Jake," said the grocer. "If you need a sack of flour and have no money to buy it, we'll give you a sack. But, see here, Jake, there's a circus coming to town in a few days, and if I give you a sack of flour, are you sure you won't sell it and take your family to the circus?"

"Oh, no!" said Jake. "I got the circus money saved up already."—*Progressive Grocer.*

WHY HE FELT SAFE

Pat was employed by a subway construction company. As he was leaving the house his wife said:

"Do mind yez don't git hurt, Pat. It's so dangerous workin' in that subway."

"Thot's all right, Biddy," replied Pat. "I borrowed two dollars from the foreman and he don't let me do any dangerous work any more."—*Selected.*

CORRECTING HIS MISTAKE

A street-car inspector was watching the work of the new conductor. "Here, Foley," he said, "how is this? You have ten passengers, and only nine fares have been rung up." "Is that so?" asked Foley. Then turning to his passengers, he yelled: "There's wan too many on this car. Git out, one of yez."

—Youth's World.

Komics

THE QUARRY

I gaze across the street so wide,
I start, I dart, I squirm, I glide,
I take my chances, oh, so slim—
I trust to eye and nerve and limb;
I scoot to right, I gallop through,
I'm here and there, I'm lost to view.
    My life, I know, hangs in the toss—
    Another plunge—I am across!
Oh, give me pity, if you can
I'm just
    a poor
        pe-des-trian.
        — *T. R. in the Boston Transcript.*

————

An elderly woman was boasting of her retentive memory. "My memory is excellent," she said. "There are only three things I can't remember. I can't remember names, and I can't remember faces, and—and I forget what the third thing is."—*The New Outlook.*

————

CONSOLATION

"Mr. Chairman," complained the speaker, stopping in his address, "I have been on my feet nearly ten minutes, but there is so much ribaldry and interruption, I can hardly hear myself speak."

"Cheer up, guv-nor," came a voice from the rear, "you ain't missin' much."—*Capper's Weekly.*

CHAPTER XII

Rome's Idolatrous Shrines

Everywhere Rome's idolatrous shrines raise their towering heads above the din and roar of the streets of our great cities, reminding us of the temples of worship in heathen lands. Millions of dollars are being expended in the construction of these great buildings. The most costly materials and equipment are being used to entice people into idolatrous worship.

The "Scarlet Mother," with her cunning and deceit, sets her incubators and hatches the brood that will finance her schemes and help to carry out her well-laid plans to grasp the reins of government and make America Catholic. To this end she has worked since the Pilgrim Fathers first landed on the Western Hemisphere, and will continue to do so until her power is broken by the education and enlightenment of the public.

When the great war-drives were on, the United States turned millions of dollars into

Rome's coffers, and it is a noticeable fact that since that time, papal structures have been going up everywhere. Besides all this, Protestants are being hoodwinked and allured into the community-chest drives, where Rome and her institutions are the greatest beneficiaries, thinking, no doubt, that they are helping the cause of humanity, when in fact they are giving their millions to finance un-American enterprises.

What are we coming to? Well might this question be asked by those who give themselves to serious thought and study. Will people who profess to be New Testament Christians continue to further the cause of popery? Will they allow Rome to get a stronger and more fatal footing in the United States? What can our leaders be thinking about? Any person, with even a slight degree of intelligence, need not be in the dark as to what the future will reveal when it may be too late to make amends. Is there no voice to cry aloud and spare not? Must the necks of the people be slipped into the noose and the knot tightened before their eyes are opened?

Through the efforts of the Knights of the Ku Klux Klan the people have received greater enlightenment than at any other period since the Lutheran Reformation. Some time ago as I passed through Atlanta, Georgia, my attention was called to Stone Mountain, where a few men who believed in Christianity and the Contitution of the United States took a solemn oath to uphold both. They pledged themselves to advocate the supremacy of the white race, a free press and free speech, and to do all within their power to protect the purity of our homes and womanhood. Why have all the imps of perdition been aroused and taken a stand against the appearance of this great patriotic organization? Why should those who have adopted their creed be so grossly misrepresented? No person has any right to citizenship in the United States who cannot uphold the principles for which this great organization stands.

Something has stirred the depths of men's souls and caused them to rise up in protest against existing conditions. Corruption is eating its way into the very heart of the nation, and unless the malady is checked, it may soon be too late. The Klansmen have seen this and are doing what they can to prevent further in-

EATING IN

roads into the heart of this great republic.

Before the breaking out of the Civil War repeated warnings were given, and had they been heeded, one of the greatest catastrophes of the ages might have been averted. But men were biased and blinded in their opinions and dominated by selfish interests. And even while the war-clouds were gathering they continued to rebel, and succeeded in plunging the nation into an awful cataclysm where hundreds of thousands had to shed their blood to uphold the sovereignty of the Federal Government. Men were presumptuous when they ought to have been on their knees in prayer. And so it is at this very hour.

Let us pray for a revival of true religion, that the consciences of men and women may be awakened. The reading of the Scriptures and the teaching of them to others should be a part of the daily program of every Christian patriot. Without divine illumination, man has been a failure in all ages. However much he may boast of his efficiency, he is unable to guide the affairs of church and state without the overruling hand of Divine Providence.

Komics

EXCOMMUNICATION

It was a wordy fight, and the little man with what looked like two pounds of sausages under his arm gave his parting shot.

"The sooner," he said, emphatically, "that I never see your face again the better it will be for both of us when he meet."—*Smith's Weekly (Sydney)*.

Komics

THREE MEANS OF GRACE

A negro preacher walked into the office of a newspaper in Rockymount, North Carolina, and said: "Misto Edito', they is forty-three of my congregation which subscribe fo' yo' paper. Do that entitle me to have a chu'ch notice in yo' Sadday issue?" "Sit down and write it," said the editor. "I thank you." And this is the notice the minister wrote: "Mount Memorial Baptist Church, the Rev. John Walker, pastor. Preaching morning and evening. In the promulgation of the gospel, three books is necessary: The Bible, the hymn-book, and the pocketbook. Come tomorrow and bring all three."—*The Christian Register.*

THE BEST COMES HIGH

Patient (nervously)—"And will the operation be dangerous, Doctor?"

Doctor—"Nonsense! You couldn't buy a dangerous operation for forty dollars."—*Life.*

SHORT WORDS PREFERRED

"If you want your parrot to talk you should begin by teaching it short words."

"That's strange. I supposed it would take quicker to polly-syllables."—*Boston Transcript.*

CHAPTER XIII

Papal Prisons in America

Should not the sixteen-foot walls around the foreign-controlled slave-pens in the United States be taken down? The ballot in the hands of enlightened men and women who know the wrongs that are being perpetrated there would cause these walls to crumble and fall. The stories that leak out from time to time, revealing the cruelties practised in these prisons, have been too well authenticated to be doubted, yet Protestants continue to help finance such institutions in the face of these facts. It is time blinded eyes were opened and deaf ears unstopped. This would result in authorizing governmental inspection of these houses so long closed to the public and to the officers of the law.

Why should there be prisons in a free country, operating under the name of charity and religion in defiance of law? What right has a police judge or any court to turn girls over to the keepers of these places for correction? They have long been under the ban of ill repute, and evidence has been given that the truth has not half been told concerning the crimes that are being perpetrated behind locks and iron bars.

The scripture says that out of the mouths of two or three witnesses every word shall be established. A vast multitude of women who have been incarcerated in these institutions have given their testimony as to what they had to suffer as unwilling inmates. Language by both tongue and pen has been exhausted by those who have tried to give details of their lives in the convents and in the so-called "Houses of the Good Shepherd," while powerless to make their escape from those who persisted in holding them in unwilling bondage. They were forbidden to write to their relatives and friends, and even when letters were allowed to be written they had to go through the hands of the censors and every word or phrase be eliminated that would give the slightest idea of discontent or ill treatment.

The imperial government that operates behind convent walls acknowledges no allegiance to the laws of the land or to governmental authorities. When a victim is once in the power of the clergy in these institutions she belongs to them, body and soul, and there is no recourse whatsoever for grievances, inasmuch as the doors are closed to anyone except to those whom the imperial heads see fit to admit.

The Mothers Superior, we are told, have their thrones in the convents and demand obeisance even to the kissing of their feet.

The crimes committed in Rome's sweatshops, where the girls have to toil under the eye of inhuman task-mistresses, are enough, if the truth were known, to cause the civilized world to revolt. The penalties meted out, as told by those who have been through the mill of experience, in many instances are not in advance of the inquisitorial methods of the Dark Ages; and often such punishment is inflicted for the slightest offenses. Can it be true that these crimes are taking place on the ground where martyrs have shed their blood in behalf of liberty?

Thank God, true American men and women are awakening, and with an all-conquering

ROME'S PRISON HOUSES MUST BE OPEN FOR
INSPECTION

spirit they will yet break the power of tyranny and lift the heel of oppression from the necks of helpless victims behind the convent walls. These houses will have an airing before the eyes of the public.

The fight is on. The awakening has come through the Knights of the Ku Klux Klan, who are even now shaking the foundations of iniquity and chasing the enemy from their refuge of lies into the open. Women also are taking a hand in this battle. Too long, through Roman Catholic teachings and practises, they have been kept in a helpless and subordinate condition. The old Roman law which made women the chattels or the slaves of men, is now in effect in this country behind the walls of papal prisons. The Roman hierarchy has succeeded for ages in keeping women in ignorance, superstition, and degradation. Many of the old Roman laws discriminating against women are still on the statute books in this country. But the franchise, or the Nineteenth Amendment to the Constitution, has placed women on a partial basis of equality and will be the means of eventually bringing them into their own. Corrupt politicians have

too long controlled the ballot-box. Women with
the ballot will help to vote down the walls of
the convents and liberate the victims of their
sex held here in galling bondage.

Our patriots are determined to hold the
fortresses of liberty. The hordes from the Old
World who have little or no love for the Stars
and Stripes will be thwarted in their design
to unite church and state and make America
Catholic.

Those who have sworn allegiance to the
Italian Pope and the flags of other countries,
while trying to exploit this nation, have much
to say about racial prejudices. God made the
races and intended that they should occupy
their own particular places on the map of the
world; and while our one hundred per
cent Americans foster hatred toward none,
they will demand their rights and will not be
intimidated by those who have the effrontery
to charge them with racial prejudice for trying
to safeguard their homes and civil liberties.

Komics

CHARACTERISTIC

Although she has an assortment of hats, she wants
new one.
(That's the woman of it.)
He says he thinks she can get along without it.
(That's the man of it.)
She insists that she can't, and she's going to get it.
(That's the woman of it.)
He says "not if he knows it."
(That's the man of it.)
She breaks down and weeps.
(That's the woman of it.)
He gives in.
(That's the end of it.)   —*Judge.*

When Tommy went visiting, his first interest was
the kitchen and what it was likely to produce. One
day, when he was visiting his grandmother, he found
her in the kitchen busy over the stove.
"What do you think I'm doing?" she asked.
Tommy shook his head and hoped hard.
"I'm going to make you a nice little pie in a sau-
cer all to yourself," said the old lady. "Don't you
think I'm good to take all that trouble?"
"Ye-es, Grandma," replied Tommy doubtfully, "of
course, it's awful good of you. But mother told me
not to be a bother, so I was just thinking that if it's

going to be any trouble p'r'aps you'd better make my pie the reg'lar size."—*Los Angeles Times.*

———

BEATING MOSE TO IT

A West Virginia Negro, a blacksmith, recently announced a change in his business as follows:

"Notice—De copoardnership heretofore resisting between me and Mose Skinner is hereby resolved. Dem what owes de firm will settle with me, and what de firm owes will settle with Mose.

———

A nodding congregation may—and may not—mean assent to what the preacher is saying.—*The Baptist.*

———

"Is your husband much of a provider, Malindy?"

"He jes' ain't nothin' else, ma'am. He gwine to git some new furniture providin' he gits de money; he gwine to git de money providin' he go to work; he go to work providin' de job suits him. I never see such a providin' man in all mah days."—*San Francisco Chronicle.*

CHAPTER XIV

Behind the Convent Walls

"Behind these cruel walls, I wait
For rescuers to come
To take me from my prison house
And to a place called home.

"I am weary of this servitude
Of misery and woe.
Deprived of liberty shall I
The joys of life e'er know?

"Is there no one who will espouse
The cause of such as I?

No one to break the power of those
Who God and state defy?

"Alas! my hope is almost gone—
Seems all to me is lost;
Yet from the winds methinks I hear
The coming of an host.

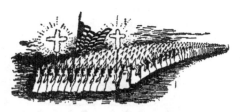

"A white-robed army brave and true
For liberty shall stand,
And from the hand of tyranny
Will break our every band.

"The fiery cross has lighted up
The nation far and wide;
They bear with them the Stars and Stripes
'Neath which our heroes ride.

"Be patient, O my soul, and wait!
Their coming draweth near;
Soon shall the rosy-tinted morn
O'er these dark walls appear.

"Why has there been no mercy shown
(Our numbers still increase)
From those who have the pow'r to make
Laws for our quick release?

"The ballot in the hands of men
With consciences awake,
Will open every prison door
And powers of darkness shake.

"Then shall the sun upon me shine
And set at liberty
All those who languish in these dens
Of dark iniquity.

"God's open Book none dare to read
Behind the convent wall,
Lest penalties be multiplied
And fear our souls appal.

"When Klansmen to the rescue come,
The Bible we shall read:
The Stars and Stripes shall o'er us wave
And ev'ry slave be freed.

"Then shall my heart in gleeful song
Come forth as from the dead,
Where once 'tween dismal walls, in gloom,
My soul on ashes fed."

CHAPTER XV

Shall the Pope Rule the World?

Loyal subjects of Rome claim the Pope to be the successor of Peter, the Vicar of Christ, the infallible god-man, the one and only Potentate that has the right to rule the nations and fix the destinies of men. Thus he would be the *one high over all* to whom the moon and the stars should bow and in reality Christ himself should have to hold a place of subordination.

The throne of the man on the Tiber is not established on the principles of good morals and of free moral agency, but on the religious and political bondage of the deluded masses from whom the Bible and Christian enlightenment are withheld. It is not difficult under this sort of Satanic delusion to build up a military machine capable of greater atrocities than have been known in by-gone ages. The whole religio-political structure is based upon falsehood, and therefore the only way it can be maintained is by the sword.

According to Rome, there are no crimes in the catalog that can baffle the infallibility of pope and priest. Multiply them a thousand fold and these confessors will grant absolution (?) if they choose to do so.

It can scarcely be conceived that in this enlightened age, nearly two thousand years after the guiding Star led the Wise Men to the manger of Bethlehem, the devil could still hold so many people in such ignorance and superstition. But such is the case. There must be a still greater struggle than the world has yet known, to defeat the forces of darkness and establish the principles of righteousness in the earth. The darkness must be dispelled by the diffusion of scriptural light.

When Jesus began His ministry, Imperial Rome had taken the place of the Republic, and Caesar was both god and king of the Romans. The soldiers from the different cities and provinces that had built up the military power had renounced their gods because they believed they were powerless to deliver them in other than their own localities; and now they worshiped Caesar, who had made great conquests by the sword. Brute force was everywhere in evidence.

THE HAND THAT WOULD GRASP THE WORLD

Caesar was lord of the world, and commander-in-chief of the Roman armies. He could lay cities waste, destroy provinces, and put to death innocent children, as well as the greatest men in the empire, if he so desired.

The representative of the Imperial Roman Government, under whom John the Baptist was put to death, was Herod Antipas. The Savior of the world was nailed to the cross by this same military power. In the agonies of death He was told by those who rejected and crucified Him that they had no king but Caesar.

This Roman imperialism still exists under the cloak of the Vatican. That the devil has not given up the conquest of this world is still manifest. The Roman Church of today with the Pope as its head is as conspicuously imperial as the Caesars of old. It is the same autocratic system that has brutalized the world in all ages and which must be supported by a military machine. It robs men of the last vestige of personal liberty and would compel them to bow to the behests of those who are the very incarnation of Satan.

God save the world from such a calamity, after rivers of blood have flowed in the price that has been paid for liberty! Subtle as a serpent are the forces that are at work trying to bring about conditions that will restore temporal power to the Pope.

That Rome wants to control the U. S. is evidenced by the following:

"His Holiness is enthusiastic over America, especially the United States. . . The Church is making advances only in America. . . . The outlook across the water is very discouraging. . . . In the midst of the gloom, abandoned by those who should stand by him in his agony, the Holy Father appeals to this country for comfort. And he appeals not in vain. American shoulders are today holding up the Vatican. Its revenues are largely derived from this country, and what is now a steady stream will soon be an overflowing river."—The *Western Watchman.*

"The question confronting this organization [German Catholic Verein] is what to do about the dangers that are now threatening Christianity (the Roman Catholic Church) in this country. In France and Portugal the Catholic Church was defeated and persecuted because the Catholics were not organized. . . . I want to say that when the time comes in this country, as it surely will come . . . they will not find us unprepared or unorganized and they shall not prevail.
"We have well ordered and efficient organizations, all at the beck and nod of the Hierarchy, and ready to do what the Church authorities tell them to do."
—Speech by Archbishop Quigley.

"He [General Miles] says that we are trying to make the United States a Catholic country. We most certainly are doing all in our power to accomplish it."—*The Catholic Register*, Apr. 16, 1924.

"Undoubtedly it is the intention of the Pope to possess this country. In this intention he is aided by the Jesuits and all the Catholic prelates and priests.—Dr. O. A. Bronson (Catholic Writer).

"The Pope has received a detailed report of the elections in America, and has learned with great satisfaction of the successes attained by a number of Catholic candidates. He is especially pleased that the governors of a half-dozen important states are Catholics."—Rome, Nov. 15, 1913.

"We have Catholic congressmen representing many districts of New York City. We wonder what they are going to do in Congress in response to the demand that the postal laws be amended in order that the anti-Catholic papers be thrown out of the mails."—*The Tablet*, Dec. 26, 1914.

CHAPTER XVI

Patriots, Hold Together!

Patriots, hold together! You have a great and glorious cause. You cannot afford to allow, at the peril of your lives and your country, the banner of one hundred per cent Americanism to be trailed in the dust, or the principles that you have so valiantly espoused to go down in ignominy and shame. Let no lack of unity in this crucial hour defeat the purpose of an all-wise God to keep America Protestant.

The great awakening that has come to the country under the leadership of the Ku Klux Klan has been so timely, spectacular, and far-reaching as to almost stagger the human mind. So marvelous has been the transformation that has come to a heretofore unenlightened public that it can be attributed to nothing less than a miracle.

It was so when the sunbeams from the throne of Mercy and Justice burst in upon an

enslaved and darkened world at the beginning
of the Lutheran Reformation. No power on
earth or in perdition has ever been able to undo what was then accomplished by a German
monk, in exposing the infamous system of
graft and corruption which operated under a
cloak of religion. The world had been cursed
for centuries in those countries where the Pope
had compelled the benighted multitudes to
bow to his mandates with the threat of excommunication, physical death, and the tor-
ments of an eternal hell.

At this stage of human progress nothing
can undo what has been accomplished by the
Knights of the Ku Klux Klan. Millions have
received enlightenment that will yet bring a
harvest in the United States, and other countries as well. Divine illumination has come to
the multitudes. Their consciences have been
awakened to a greater conception of the principles of good government and the sacrifices
that bring it about.

If patriotism should be allowed to die in
the United States, civilization would go
and Christianity would perish from the earth.
To be indifferent to the issues we are now fac-

ing would show that the heart is estranged to the principles of justice, truth, and honesty.

In the last general election (1925) men were swept into office as governors of some of the states by the European hordes who were dominated by the old Roman Catholic machine. This was done in the name of a "holy religion" or of the so-called "infallible" pope. The scripture says, "Woe unto them that call evil good, and good evil; that put darkness for light, and light for darkness; that put bitter for sweet, and sweet for bitter" (Isa. 5:20).

In every good and great cause there have always been traitors,—men who have sold out to the powers of evil for gold or to gratify their personal ambition. But we cannot afford to lay down our weapons of warfare because of what others may do, and allow the cause to fail. Our only safety is in eternal vigilance, and a disposition to overlook the faults and failures of our fellow patriots when not of a serious character.

Rome never slumbers. She uses every device of Satanic power to hold her deluded and illiterate followers together. Autocracy has been her arm of strength by which she has

"MARCH ROUND AND ROUND, BLOW LONG   AND LOUD,
THE WALLS ARE FALLING DOWN."

forced her will upon her subjects, who have been made to believe that when the Pope speaks, God is speaking; when he commands, God is commanding.

From the *Catholic Weekly* of New York is quoted the following:

"We are Catholics first, last, and all the time. Our career is to enlighten Catholics of every nationality and to defend the Church against every comer no matter who or what he is. When the Pope speaks the Church speaks, God speaks. Though we love our country dearly we love our Church more."

From the *Tablet*, another Roman Catholic paper, is quoted:

"The Roman Catholic citizens of the United States owe no allegiance to the principles of the Government which is condemned by the Pope."

And, again, we quote from the *Catholic Review*:

"When a Catholic candidate is on the ticket and his opponent is a non-Catholic, let the Catholic have the vote, no matter what he represents."

Shall we as Protestants allow dissensions and divisions to creep into our ranks? Shall the public continue to be deceived in the face of such revelations of Rome's diabolical schemes to sieze the reins of power and bring on another inquisition?

If such expressions were found in Protestant papers, editors and publishers would be convicted of high treason. The hierarchy openly declares that the Church has the right to exercise its authority without having any limits set to it by the civil powers; that the Church has the right to avail herself of force and to use the temporal power for that purpose; also that her priests have the right to immunity from all civil laws. From another publication the following is quoted:

"The clergy should be tried for civil and criminal offenses only in ecclesiastical courts."

And again:

"Public Schools, open to all children for the education of the young, should be under the control of the Church and should not be subject to civil power nor made to conform to the opinions of the age."

This is only a drop in the ocean of the sentiment that is being expressed by the Roman Catholic press showing the trend of the hierarchy's activity and ambition. Every person who has any conception of liberty should be willing to make a sacrifice to help withstand the powers that are now threatening our national life.

Sectionalism is a mighty foe to human progress, and men of clear vision and broad mind should not permit themselves to be dominated by it. Some so-called patriots confine their operations to the town and county in which they live. They have scarcely been broad enough to consider the state in which they live and its interests, much less the forty-eight states that comprise the Union over which waves the Stars and Stripes. We cannot afford to be persons of parsimonious minds in the face of a national and world crisis. Again we exhort the patriots to stand together, and let not the enemy rob them of their God-given heritage!

————

"Stand fast therefore in the liberty wherewith Christ hath made us free, and be not entangled again with the yoke of bondage."   Galatians 5:1.

DON'T TOUCH THE EAGLE'S NEST

THE PRINCIPLES OF THE KU KLUX KLAN

The principles of the Ku Klux Klan can best be expressed briefly by giving to my readers "A Klansman's Kreed" with a few added words of explanation.

"I believe in God and in the tenets of the Christian religion, and that a godless nation cannot long prosper."

The Christian religion is founded on the teachings of Jesus Christ. An infidel, or a person who rejects Jesus Christ and His teachings, cannot be a true Klansman. And the nation that rejects God and His word is sure to reap calamity of some kind.

"I believe that a Church that is not grounded on the principles of morality and justice is a mockery to God and to man."

There are churches, so-called, that do not require a high standard of morality and justice from their membership. Men who accept

153

the teachings of such churches cannot be Klansmen, in the true sense of the word. The genuine Christian is both moral and just.

"I believe that a Church that does not have the welfare of the common people at heart is unworthy."

Any Church that is founded on the principles set forth in the teachings of Jesus Christ has the welfare of all people at heart. There is no class distinction, no subjection of the masses by a favored few, as has been the case for centuries in Mexico and other Romanized countries.

"I believe in the eternal separation of Church and State."

Roman Catholicism teaches the union of Church and State, with the Church controlling the State. The Constitution of the United States declares that Church and State shall forever be separate. The Church has its function, which is spiritual; the State its function, which is temporal. Each has its place, and while they should work in harmony, they should be separate.

"I hold no allegiance to any foreign government, emperor, king, pope, or any other foreign political or religious power."

Every Roman Catholic holds allegiance to the Pope of Rome, and Catholicism teaches that this allegiance is superior to his allegiance to his country.

"I believe in just laws and liberty."

By just laws is meant laws that apply equally to all, rich and poor, educated and uneducated, men and women.

Liberty does not mean license, as many seem to think. It does not mean to do as one pleases regardless of others; it means that in the exercise of our privilege the welfare of others and of society at large must be considered.

"I hold my allegiance to the Stars and Stripes next to my allegiance to God:"

God should be honored and obeyed above all. But next to Him we should hold allegiance to the Stars and Stripes, the emblem of our liberties.

"I believe in the upholding of the Constitution of these United States."

By upholding the Constitution is meant the whole Constitution including the Eight-

PUSH HIM OFF

eenth Amendment. One who would violate one clause of the Constitution would just as quickly break every other one if it served his purpose to do so.

"I believe that our free public school is the corner-stone of good government, and that those who are seeking to detroy it are enemies of our Republic and are unworthy of citizenship."

Ignorance, superstition, immorality and crime go together. Destroy our public schools and the rule of our country will be placed in the hands of the few, as is the case where there are no public schools. There are enemies within our gates who are trying to break down our system of education and substitute therefor a Church-controlled system which would put more stress on church dogma than general education. The result would be the ignorant masses controlled by the educated few.

"I believe in freedom of speech."

By this is meant the right of any citizen to express an opinion on any subject, either publicly or privately, so long as no other person's private character is assailed. Until the arising of the Ku Klux Klan, this right was denied American citizens in many cities and towns.

"I believe in a free press, uncontrolled by political parties or religious sects."

The press should be free to spread news without coloring it to suit any person, party or sect, but such is not the case. Scarcely a newspaper anywhere dares to publish the truth, the whole truth and nothing but the truth. The press is largely controlled by the Roman Catholic priesthood and the Jewish advertisers. As a result, the people are fed on propaganda instead of truth. When an article is read in either a newspaper or magazine, one does not know but what there is a sinister motive back of it. And a paper that publishes the truth can hardly exist.

"I believe in law and order."

In other words, the Klan believes in keeping the laws and in enforcing the laws,—the Prohibition law as well as others. Many accusations have been brought against the Klan as law-breakers. These accusations against the order are newspaper propaganda. So far we have not heard of a single instance where the Klan, by an official act, has violated any law.

"I believe in white supremacy."

The Klan believes that America is a white man's country and should be governed by white men.   Yet the Klan is not anti-negro; it is the negro's friend.   The Klan is eternally opposed to the mixing of the white and colored races.   Their creed is: Let the white man remain white, the black man black, the yellow man yellow, the brown man brown and the red man red.   God drew the color line and man should so let it remain.

"I believe in the protection of our pure womanhood."

This is a stand for the purity of the home, for morality, for the protection of our mothers, our sisters, our wives, our daughters, against the white-slaver, the home-wrecker, the libertine.   To live up to this principle a Klansman must keep himself pure; he must treat other woman as he would have those of his own household treated.

POOR CAMOUFLAGE

"I do not believe in mob violence, but I do believe that laws should be enacted to prevent the cause of mob violence."

Deaths by mob violence have fallen off very materially since the advent of the Klan. The Klan believes in law-enforcement, and if a person has committed a crime the law should take its course.

"I believe in a closer relationship of capital and labor."

Instead of being antagonistic one toward the other, capital and labor should work in harmony. This would be the case if men observed the teachings of Christ in His word, and if they would observe the teachings embodied in the Klan motto, *Non silba sed anthar*—Not for self but for others.

"I believe in the prevention of unwarranted strikes by foreign labor agitators."

Many strikes, if traced to their origin, will be found to have been originated by some foreign agitator, not by the laboring men themselves. Very few strike agitators are American born.

FOOLING HIMSELF BUT NO ONE ELSE

"I believe in the limitation of foreign immigration."

No nation can absorb an unlimited number of foreigners and retain its national integrity and traditions. Immigration should be controlled by the nation which the immigrants are entering. That nation should be the judge as to whom it will receive. The traditions of America have well-nigh been buried under the avalanche of foreign ideas and ideals. But for the arising of the Ku Klux Klan, they would now have been but a memory in some parts of our country.

"I am a native born American citizen and I believe my rights in this country are superior to those of foreigners."

The Klan believes in England for Englishmen, France for Frenchmen, Italy for Italians, and America for Americans. Is there anything objectionable in this? The Klan is not anti-Catholic, anti-Jew, anti-Negro, anti-foreign; it is pro-Protestant and pro-American.

The Klan does not oppose the foreigner who comes to our shores and becomes an

American citizen and an American at heart, but it does oppose those who come here to drag America down to the level of the priest-ridden countries of Southern Europe, while hoarding up good American dollars and living under the protection of American laws.

THE END

■ ■

ALMA COLLEGE

ZAREPHATH, N. J.

Bishop Alma White, A. M., Founder
Rev. Arthur K. White, A. M., Dean

Alma College was founded for the purpose of promoting the interests of Christian culture and education. It is one of the few

CO-EDUCATIONAL

institutions of the eastern section of the United States. Our object is to inculcate in the hearts and minds of young men and women, along with their educational training, a profound respect for law and order as embodied in the administrations of our government, a deep regard for the sanctity of the home, which is the foundation stone of our American civilization, and a heartfelt reverence for the Bible and the religion of Jesus Christ.

Alma College is accredited by the State Board of Education of New Jersey.

Catalog giving full information as to requirements for entrance, courses, expense, etc., sent upon application. Address:

Alma College,   **Zarephath, N. J.**

■ ■

GENERAL VIEW OF ZAREPHATH'S BUILDINGS

PILLAR OF FIRE COLLEGE BUILDING, DENVER, COLORADO

ALMA PREPARATORY SCHOOL
ZAREPHATH, N, J.

Bishop Alma White, A. M., Founder
Rev. Arthur K. White, A. M., Dean

(Registered by the State Board of Education)

A four years' Academy course is given in this school, preparing students for college. The work done is of a very high standard, equal to that of the best high schools in the state.

Catalog giving full information sent on application.

ADDRESS:

Alma Preparatory School,   Zarephath, N. J.

ZAREPHATH BIBLE INSTITUTE
ZAREPHATH, N. J.

Bishop Alma White, A. M., Founder
Rev. Ray B. White, A. M., President

Established for the training of preachers, evangelists, and missionaries. Free from the taint of higher criticism and evolution. A three and a four years' course of study, equipping the student for efficient service in the vineyard of the Lord.

Catalog sent free on application. Address:

Zarephath Bible Institute,   Zarephath, N. J.

■■■■■■■■■■■■■■■■■■■■■■■

BELLEVIEW JUNIOR COLLEGE,

ACADEMY, and BIBLE INSTITUTE

DENVER, COLO.

(Church, 1847 Champa St., Denver, Colorado)

Bishop Alma White, A. M., Founder
Rev. Ray B. White, A. M., President

This school, consisting of three departments, Junior College, Academy, and Bible Institute, is conducted on the same general principles as the schools located at Zarephath, New Jersey.

It is situated on College Hill, a remarkable surburban plateau seven miles from the business center of Denver, the Queen City of the West. A more ideal spot could not be found. The towering, snow-clad peaks of the Rockies for a distance of more than two hundred miles north and south are plainly visible on the west, while the great plains stretch out toward the east. The views from the tower of the main building are indescribable. One of the most healthful spots to be found on the globe, and extraordinarily unique as a location for a Christian school.

Write for catalog.

Belleview Junior College, 1845 Champa St.,
Denver, Colorado.

■■■■■■■■■■■■■■■■■■■■■

168

The Ku Klux Klan in Prophecy

Contains 19 chapters, 148 pages, portrait of the author and 22 striking cartoons. Also explanation of the Principles of the Ku Klux Klan.

The chapter headings are as follows:

Rome in Prophecy—The Bible Description of the Pope—The 20th Century Reformation—A New Star Baffles Rome—Enemies of the Ku Klux Klan Striken with Blindness—Jonah, the Jew—A Fugitive from God—Gideon's Army of 100 Percenters—Feeding the Multitudes—The Good Samaritan—Bow or Burn—Rome in Control of City Governments—Papal Contention for Rulership of the World—A Patriot's Prayer—Rome Intercepted—The Axe Laid at the Root of the Papal Tree—The Protectors of True Americanism—The Iron Hand of the Pope in Mussolini's Government—Great Klan Victory in the Election of 1924—The Ku Klux Klan and Woman's Cause.

The Introduction to this book is by Arthur H. Bell, Grand Dragon, Realm of New Jersey, Knights of the Ku Klux Klan.

Price, 50c., Postpaid

Write us for special prices to Klaverns

ADDRESS

The Good Citizen,   Zarephath, N. J.

Books by Bishop Alma White

LOOKING BACK FROM BEULAH (English and German)
Thousands have been strengthened by reading it, and in-
spired to holier living. 350 pages. Price, $1, postpaid.

THE NEW TESTAMENT CHURCH (2 vols.)—These two
volumes show the reader what constitutes the true Church.
Price, 50¢ each volume, postpaid.

THE CHOSEN PEOPLE—Treats on the restoration of Israel, and the two works of grace—Justification and Sanc-
tification. Price, 75¢, postpaid.

RESTORATION OF ISRAEL, THE HOPE OF THE
WORLD—This important Bible doctrine is clearly shown
from New Testament types. Price, 60¢, postpaid.

TRUTH STRANGER THAN FICTION—This book is a
great revelation to its readers. Shows God's dealings with
those who rejected His word. Price, 60¢, postpaid.

MY TRIP TO THE ORIENT—An intensely interesting account of the author's trip to Egypt and Palestine. Illustrated. Price 75¢, postpaid.

WITH GOD IN THE YELLOWSTONE—A description of the
author's trip through the Yellowstone National Park. Over
40 illustrations, 5 in colors. Price, 75c., postpaid.

THE TITANIC TRAGEDY—GOD SPEAKING TO THE
NATIONS—Contains a message to the nations—especially
Great Britain. Illustrated. Price, $1, postpaid.

THE VOICE OF NATURE—This book, written in verse, will
direct your mind to God's great out-of-doors. Lessons from
grass, flowers, trees, birds, animals. Illustrated. Cloth, 75c.,
postpaid.

LIFE SKETCHES—Concise review of the Author's earlier life.
Written in verse. Illustrated. Cloth, 75c., postpaid.

Pillar of Fire,   Zarephath, N. J.

172

Books by Bishop Alma White

MY HEART AND MY HUSBAND—A historical poem representing certain phases of the author's experiences during the past thirty years. Intensely interesting. Strikingly illustrated. Price, 50c, postpaid. Order from Alma White, Zarephath, N. J.

WHY I DO NOT EAT MEAT—Discusses the subject of eating animal flesh from both a scriptural and a hygienic standpoint. Original drawings. Price, 50¢, postpaid.

DEMONS AND TONGUES—Tells about the origin and workings of the "Tongues" movement. Price, 15¢, postpaid.

GOLDEN SUNBEAMS—A marvelous book for young people. A great character builder. Price, 70c., postpaid.

GEMS OF LIFE—The children's book. Short, original stories and poems. Illustrated. Price, 60c., postpaid.

By Other Authors

YOUR HOME YOUR COLLEGE or "Throughly Furnished"— By Rev. Arthur K. White, A. M.—A "golden treasury of knowledge." Illustrated. 290 pages. Price, $1.50, postpaid.

A CHALLENGE FROM THE PULPIT—By Rev. Ray B. White, A. M.—A heart appeal to men and women. Illustrated. 240 pages. Price, $1, postpaid.

THE LEGEND OF MANITOUSA—POEMS AND SKETCHES (including "Hank," a story that will make you laugh), by Rev. Ray B. White, A. M. The poem "Manitousa," breathes the spirit of the Indians and the great Western plains. Pen drawings. Cloth, $1, postpaid.

THE HARP OF GOLD—This book has an important place in the Gospel of song. For use in the church, Sunday-school, revival meetings, etc. Price, bristol, 20c.; cloth, 30c., postpaid.

THE SILVER TRUMPET—A new song book, containing more than 300 songs, together with selected Psalms, promises, etc. Many new songs never published before and a large number of the old favorites; a male quartette section and a children's section. Suitable for all religious services and patriotic meetings. Price, cloth, 50c., postpaid; $40 a hundred, not prepaid.

Pillar of Fire,   Zarephath, N. J.

Periodicals Edited by Bishop Alma White

PILLAR OF FIRE—A 16-page journal devoted to the interests of the Christian life. The very best religious paper for earnest Christians; deeply spiritual. Weekly. $1.25 a year.

THE GOOD CITIZEN—A 16-page monthly magazine dealing with social, political, and religious questions concerning the nations. It is a live American paper. 50c. a year.

PILLAR OF FIRE JUNIOR—This paper is devoted to the interests of the young people. Contains just the articles the children need. Eight-page weekly. 50c. a year.

WOMAN'S CHAINS—A magazine devoted to the cause of woman. A staunch champion of her rights in church and state—rights she does not fully enjoy. Sixteen pages. Issued every two months. Subscription price, 50c. a year.

THE ROCKY MOUNTAIN PILLAR OF FIRE—A practical religious journal. It stands for the highest ideals. Official organ of the Pillar of Fire in the Rocky Mountain region. Semi-monthly, $1 a year. Address, 1845 Champa St., Denver, Colo.

OCCIDENTAL PILLAR OF FIRE—A deeply spiritual paper, published in the interest of the Pillar of Fire work on the Pacific coast. Semi-monthly. Sixteen pages. Subscription price, $1 a year. Address, Pillar of Fire, 1185 E. Jefferson St., Los Angeles, California.

LONDON PILLAR OF FIRE—A full salvation monthly. Gives interesting accounts of the Pillar of Fire work abroad. The articles touch every phase of the Christian life. 75c. a year. Order through this office.

THE BRITISH SENTINEL—Exposes the dangers which threaten Great Britain. Deals with corrupt politics, the questions of the day, etc. 75c. a year. Order through this office.

Pillar of Fire,   Zarephath, N. J.

CPSIA information can be obtained at www.ICGtesting.com
Printed in the USA
BVOW08s0026170714

359425BV00023B/626/P